ENTERING NORTH CAROLINA

SET CLOCKS BACK 100 YEARS

Jim Leutze

For information contact Triton Press/Nautilus Publishing, 426 South Lamar Blvd., Suite 16, Oxford, MS 38655.

ISBN: 978-1-936-946-37-2

Triton Press
A division of The Nautilus Publishing Company
426 South Lamar Blvd., Suite 16
Oxford, Mississippi 38655
Tel: 662-513-0159
www.nautiluspublishing.com
www.JimLeutze.com

First Edition

Front cover illustration by Dwane Powell

Library of Congress Cataloging-in-Publication Data has been applied for.

10   9   8   7   6   5   4   3   2   1

For my children
and my grandchildren Eliza, Travis, Sam, Parker and Sara Kate,
all of whom live in and hope for a brighter future in North Carolina.

CONTENTS

PREFACE

Some people have asked why I wrote this book and specifically why I am so outraged. I am one of the North Carolinians who chose to live in the state in the 1960s because of its ongoing improvements to the quality of life for all its citizens. I was born in Charleston, South Carolina, where my father was stationed at Parris Island, and I have roots in more than one region. My father was from Savannah, my mother from Vermont, and after our stay in South Carolina, I was raised in a conservative section of Maryland. From an early age, I wearied of the old clichés about southerners: they were hicks, they were backward, they were rubes, and they were racists. While there was some truth in these assumptions, it seemed grossly unfair to characterize a whole region in such damning terms. As I grew older, I learned that an African American had been lynched on the courthouse lawn in 1935 in the town where I was living. If that weren't enough to open my eyes to the ugly side of southern life, the police arrested a black man who was working on our farm and beat him senseless on *suspicion* of stealing a dog. Still I couldn't accept that all southerners were cut from the same cloth. At the University of Maryland I joined a southern fraternity, but the only insensitive thing we did was put on a minstrel show and a plantation-themed ball. But remember, these were the days of Amos and Andy.

For graduate school, my choice was Duke University. I chose it in part because it was close to the University of North Carolina at Chapel Hill, where I hoped to end up as a history professor. Also, the state's public and private universities had a national reputation for quality, which would benefit my children. Although only eight miles apart, there was a world of difference between Chapel Hill and Durham, the home of Duke. In Durham, the KKK still staged pitiful marches, while Chapel Hill was the epitome of a forward-looking town. Howard Lee, the first African American mayor in a predominantly white southern town since Reconstruction, was elected there in 1969.

I entered Duke in the fall of 1964. Through work as a staffer for Senator Hubert Humphrey, I had gotten to know North Carolina Senator B. Everett Jordan, who wanted me to meet the governor of the state where I was entering graduate school. At Jordan's request, I soon received an invitation to call on Governor Terry Sanford.

Sanford had been close to President John Kennedy, and was considered a groundbreaking southern statesman. The day on which I arrived in November 1964 was not a good time for a student to pop in. I recall Governor Sanford, who was clearing out his office, literally throwing books into boxes. After taking a few deep breaths he sat down and explained his anger. His choice for his successor, the modernizer Richardson Preyer, had been defeated when the segregationist judge, I. Beverly Lake, endorsed Preyer's opponent, Dan K. Moore. Sanford saw this election as a great step backward and a repudiation of his years of hard work. He was mad at Lake, but also at the people of North Carolina who couldn't see that they should be turning their backs on all that the segregationists represented.

After graduation, I did go to Chapel Hill as a history professor, convinced that Sanford's ideas were to be the future of North Carolina. In my enthusiasm, I co-founded the L.Q.C. Lamar Society, named for the 19th century Mississippi statesman who advocated reconciliation between North and South after the Civil War. The Society was based on the belief that the South had unparalleled opportunities if southerners could see beyond their racist past. In 1971, Governor Sanford, then president of Duke University, laid down a challenge at the L.Q.C. Lamar Society meeting in Atlanta. He said that North Carolina was about to come into its own. He referred to the reasons the South should grow and prosper – untapped natural and human resources, a benign climate, an exemplary work ethic, a developing infrastructure... and now, "what was so vital, a people not preoccupied with maintaining the old southern status quo based on race and class." It was vindication; I had chosen the right state in which to live and raise a family; the clichés about the region were myths of the past, not the future. North Carolina, with its climate, its natural beauty, its fine higher education system and its growing economy, could become an example of a modern society not only to the South, but to the nation.

For the next 40 years, the state generally followed the path advocated by Sanford and those who followed him. Progress continued — in 1950 we were 44th in the nation in per capita income; in 1990 we were 36th. In 1980 our per capita income was $600 less than Louisiana's and by 1990 it was $2,000 more. Between 1990 and 2000 North Carolina's per capita income grew 17.3 percent compared to a national rate of 11.4 percent. Still, we lagged the national average by approximately 2.5 percent from 2008 to 2010. We were making progress, but still had a ways to go. Then, in 2010, something dramatic happened: traditionalist politicians who campaigned as Republicans took over the state legislature and, in 2012 the governorship, vowing to bring change. But what change?

In a paroxysm of traditionalism, the Republicans went after abortion, voter registrations, public employees — including teachers — environmental regulations, Medicaid, the earned income tax credit, and virtually anything associated with Obama, Jim Hunt, Marc Basnight, and the Democratic Party and its perceived socialism. It was a giant leap backward. Once, North Carolina had compared itself to Virginia or other states we thought were making progress; now we compare ourselves to South Carolina or Mississippi. What happened to my cherished, modernizing North Carolina? What is happening to education here? After a career as an educator — professor of history, UNC-Chapel Hill; president, Hampden-Sydney College; chancellor, UNC-Wilmington — and candidate for the North Carolina Senate in 2010, I am particularly angry about the shabby treatment of our teachers and our schools. The new Republican leadership seems to have a perverse inclination to verify all the old clichés about the backwards South. I want my state back!

The story that follows is an effort to fill in the six million North Carolinians who have come here since 1960 on where we came from – and to alert all of the state's population to where we seem to be going. We are currently in the process of compiling our updated report to see how life in North Carolina will change if the current policies are put into full effect. Finally, I will propose <u>how</u> those who love the "old North Carolina" can take our state back.

It is also hoped that by understanding historical background, unaffiliated voters, independent voters and disenchanted Republicans and Democrats can be convinced that they don't want to return to the past. Only through a coalition of moderate voters can the state return to a forward direction. I hope this book will provide them with a roadmap to a better future.

INTRODUCTION

For those who were born or came here in the last four decades of the 20th Century, North Carolina seemed a relatively forward-looking state, with its emphasis on education, research, environment, good government and good roads. Then in 2010 and again in 2012, North Carolinians got a surprise. After 150 years of sporadic forward movement, North Carolina began a policy of astonishing deconstruction.

A state that had slowly dug itself out of poverty and negative stereotypes began suddenly to go backward in time, with the election of committed conservatives in the Governor's Office and conservatives as the ruling majority in the state legislature. This is a story of stunning negativity with national implications. If North Carolina can make a 180-degree turn, what can be said for other states that haven't so painfully pulled themselves up from the mire of slave-ocracy and the repression of the rights of working people? What are businessmen in North Carolina thinking? What are business interests in the country thinking? Is this a state to which they wish to come? Is this a portent of the future?

In the 2014 elections we may get our first answer to that last question. Should the Republicans gain control of both the U.S. House and the Senate, we may see played out in Washington what we have seen played out in Raleigh over the past four years. The battle between Kay Hagan and Thom Tillis will help determine that future.

It is my contention that the Republican Party, Tea Party and some very conservative out-of-state interests targeted North Carolina in 2010 as a test case for their conservative agenda. Recognizing that North Carolina has always had a strong traditionalist strain despite our modernist reputation, they realized that with sufficient organizing and funding, North Carolina could be turned from pale Blue to deep Red. In that election they took over both houses of the North Carolina General Assembly, while in 11 states they took control of both the legislative and elective branches. There are now 20 such states. North Carolina is now considered to have one of the most conservative legislatures in the country. Once in control of the North Carolina General Assembly, they were in control of drawing legislative districts, and thus control of our congressional delegation; once in control of the courts, they were in control of regulations. One measure of their success is that North Carolina has enacted the strictest voter repression policies in the country, instated a flat tax, and abolished teacher tenure (recently delayed by court order) as part of an attack on public schools. The same tactics could be used in other states, particularly where there is a large number of working-class voters; Pennsylvania, Michigan, Ohio, Illinois and Wisconsin are all being targeted, and Pennsylvania has already adopted a voter registration law that the Republican legislature leaders admitted was intended to reduce the turnout of Democratic voters.

The Republican/Tea Party playbook obviously worked out in this state in part because of the continuing legacy of the famously right-wing U.S. Senator Jesse Helms and one rich man who longed to be a national political force — Art Pope. Thus a state once seen as the model for the New South became the poster child for a radical orthodoxy.

And one thing needs to be made clear: while these political leaders claim that this is the first time in a century that the Republicans have held power in North Carolina, that is only true because this is a different Republican party. In short, their claim is a distinction without a difference. The views and policies of these Republicans are most similar to the traditionalist Democrats who took power in the state in 1898. These Democrats held unchallenged power at least until the 1950s. The current Republicans could hardly be called the Party of Lincoln or even the Party of Eisenhower; they are more the Party of McKinley, with more than a pinch of Tea Party Know-Nothingism.

Now each state is obviously different, but this book shows how the takeover was accomplished, the historical themes that are repeating themselves, and what needs to be done to restore North Carolina and other states facing similar threats to a forward course.

HISTORIC THEMES

A careful review of North Carolina history reveals several important themes:

• We have followed a pattern of <u>one step forward, two steps back</u>. This illustrates how finely divided the state has always been. Whichever group has been in power, there always has been an opposition just beneath the surface. Modernizing tendencies have always faced resistance, and when that resistance has been in power it has taken the form of revisiting our worst policies and displaying our worst instincts, including racism, anti-intellectualism, misogyny and xenophobia.

• At various points in our history we have turned to <u>voter suppression</u>, using the land holding status, race, or gender that the traditionalists have used to limit the vote.

• As the foregoing shows, there has always been a <u>strong conservative strain</u> in North Carolina; even progressive leaders have had to guard against going too far too fast.

• <u>The power of the business community</u>. Although they have varied over time from large landowners to industrialists to bankers to insurance magnates, they have had a disproportionate influence on North Carolina's direction.

• <u>The role of education</u>. Modernizers always saw public education as a democratizing essential and an economic energizer. Traditionalists have been less supportive. They equate education with elitism and see it as giving legitimacy to radical ideas.

• Low taxes: they have often been the tool to limit educational opportunity and appeal to the business community.

• North Carolina has seen a succession of political dynasties. These dynasties were led by powerful individuals who were followed by their acolytes. This has been true from Zebulon Vance to O. Max Gardner to Jesse Helms.

• Coalitions. To overthrow the political party in power, it has been necessary to form coalitions as the Fusionists did in 1894. The current coup occurred when the traditional Republicans formed a coalition with business and the Tea Party.

TERMINOLOGY

Writers have long struggled with how to characterize North Carolina in political terms. *Conservative, liberal, reactionary, progressive* have all been tried, but no one term seems to suffice. A political scientist, Paul Luebke, who also serves in the North Carolina House of Representatives, has written an analysis that should be borne in mind:

> "Despite North Carolina's long-standing reputation for progressiveness, the term 'progressive' should be applied cautiously. The reality is that the state's political debate remains firmly controlled by two well-institutionalized economic elites with somewhat conflicting interests. One group, the modernizers, consists of bankers, developers, retail merchants, the news media and other representatives of the business community who expect to benefit from change and growth. The second group includes the traditionalists, includes traditional industrialists (in textiles, furniture and apparel) tobacco farmers, and others associated with the agricultural economy who feel threatened by change and growth. Each group is linked with politicians who represent its interests." (Luebke VIII)

Although Luebke was speaking primarily about the 20th century, I think the terms are also appropriate for movements and people in the 19th century. So, for the purpose of this manuscript, I will use "modernizer" and "traditionalist," and let the reader make whatever other distinction they wish. After 2010, though, I will call the traditionalists "redeemers" after their white supremacist forebears in 1898 whom they clearly resemble.

Then there is the matter of political parties. Our story begins before there was a Republican Party. In the 1830s, 40s and 50s the Whigs most closely represented what would later become the Republicans. They favored public education, internal improvements and modernization in general. By 1860 they had fractured, but the Constitutional Union Party took up many Whig issues and ran an anti-secession candidate for president. That candidate lost by only 4,000 votes, thus illustrating how badly North Carolina was torn in the period leading up to the Civil War.

After the war, the Republicans, who were modernizers, ran the state only from 1865 to 1871. Some former Whigs joined the Republicans but were known by the Democratic opposition as "Scalawags." At the time of the Civil War and after the Democratic Party was the pro-slavery, secessionist, traditionalist party. They took control from the Republicans during the period 1871 to 1894 and then from 1898 through 2010. In the mid-20th Century, they were not pro-slavery, but many Democrats opposed civil rights and some could be called racists. During part of this time, there were some Democrats, particularly in Eastern North Carolina who were called "Jessecrats," meaning Democrats who supported Republican Jesse Helms in part, at least, for his views on race. This was primarily a result of the Nixonian Southern Strategy. Nixon saw in the Civil Rights Act of 1964 and Voting Rights Act of 1965 an opportunity to pry the South out of the Democratic column. Relying on the lingering white supremacist sentiment in the South, the Republican Party positioned itself to the right of the Democrats. It worked, as the Republicans became the traditionalists, leaving the modernizers to the Democrats.

This strategy fractured North Carolina, although many Republicans never totally bought into the traditionalists' mantra. These Republicans were suspicious of big government, unenthusiastic about many regulations, and while generally opposed to higher taxes, they were supportive of public education and a modern infrastructure. Governors James Holshouser and James Martin were both representative of this group.

The definitional problem continues. Recent headlines note that Thom Tillis won the 2014 Republican primary for the "establishment." This is despite the fact that Tillis describes himself as an archconservative. *The Economist* magazine titled its story about the North Carolina election with a headline, "The Establishment Wins — Sort Of."

It is my contention that the current group of Republicans represents a break from the recent past. If they resemble anything historically, they would be Democrats from the 1880s and 1890s. Yet even that does not capture their unique nature. They combine something of the old Democrats with a generous mixture of Libertarianism. At present what they want to build is not as clear as what they want to tear down. As someone has observed, "low taxes aren't a policy."

NOTE ON SOURCES

This is not a work of original scholarship. I have relied on a range of books and articles, but those listed below were particularly helpful. I also used state and federal sources for economic data.

W. J. Cash, *The Mind of the South* (Alfred Knopf, 1941).

William Chafe, *Civilities and Civil Rights* (Oxford University Press, 1981).

Rob Christensen, *The Paradox of North Carolina Politics* (UNC Press, Chapel Hill 2008).

Lee Craig, *Josephus Daniels* (UNC Press, Chapel Hill, 2013).

Robert Durden, *The Dukes of Durham: 1865-1929* (Duke University Press, 1975).

Tom Eamons, *The Making of a Southern Democracy* (UNC Press, Chapel Hill, 2013).

V. O. Key, *Southern Politics in State & Nation* (Alfred Knopf, 1949).

Hugh Talmade Lefler & Ray Newsome, *North Carolina: History of a Southern State* (UNC Press, Chapel Hill, 1973).

Paul Luebke, *Tar Heel Politics, 2000* (UNC Press, Chapel Hill, 2001).

Gary Pearce, *Jim Hunt, A Biography* (John F. Blair, 2010).

William Pleasants & Agustus Burnsill, *Frank Porter Graham & the 1990 Senate Race* (UNC Press, Chapel Hill, 1990).

William Powell, *North Carolina Through Four Centuries* (UNC Press, Chapel Hill, 1989).

LeRae S. Umfleet, *A Day of Blood: The 1898 Wilmington Race Riot* (Raleigh, NC Office of Archives & History, 2009).

C. Van Woodward, *Origins of the New South: 1877-1913* (LSU Press, Baton Rouge, 1951)

I also conducted a number of interviews and received numerous helpful comments from readers of drafts of this book. Out of respect for their privacy and to avoid embarrassment, I shall not list their names. All opinions, conclusions and errors are mine and mine alone.

This book could not have been completed without the support of my wife, Margaret Gates and my long-time executive assistant, Lynne Goodspeed.

CHAPTER I
"FROM DAWN TO DUSK" 1815 - 1876

North Carolina was long known as a poor, rural southern state divided geographically and by class. Some, derisively, referred to it as the "Rip van Winkle" state, after the fictional villager who took a twenty-year nap. The East was home to the planter aristocracy, such as it was, and the Piedmont and the Mountains were home to the yeoman farmers. Early in the 19th century, a public-spirited citizen, unhappy with the status quo, proposed a bold scheme to vault North Carolina into the forefront of southern states. Archibald D. Murphey of Hillsborough was a lawyer, lawmaker, jurist, planter and early entrepreneur. He realized that the people of the state were largely poor, backward, and ignorant. Feeling strongly that the quickest way to turn the state around was to improve the lives of its people, he began gathering statistics and informing himself on how their condition might be advanced.

Between 1815 and 1818 Murphey made a series of reports characterizing the state's problems and proposing a list of ways to improve. His plan included public schools, internal improvements, a new constitution, and reclaiming land currently unsuitable for agriculture. A major feature of his plan was to vastly improve the communication system. He saw roads, bridges, canals and other internal improvements as key to the economic development of the state. Moreover, if properly designed, these communication routes could help unify the people of the state and connect them with markets and ideas. In addition, the increased revenue would be available to underwrite a public education system.

His plan was sweeping and revolutionary – too sweeping and revolutionary, particularly for the powerful political forces in the East. Their natural conservatism was reinforced by the economic downturn of 1819, whereupon it became easy to play the "lack of resources" card. Consequently, most of Murphy's dream was not to be pursued, although there was a push for more roads, plank roads — some of which required tolls — and an improved system of dams and locks on the numerous rivers.

Murphey's thinking was an inspiration to a whole group of young leaders who eagerly bought in to Murphey's vision. According to one historian, "The most revolutionary feature of the new movement was its repudiation of the prevalent philosophy that government is a necessary evil and its bold acceptance of the concept that a democratic government is the servant of the people and their most effective agency for self-development."(Lefler, ibid) This same historian found Murphey's work to have "laid the foundations of the present modern commonwealth." (Lefler, 328)

It took almost two decades before the effects of the Murphey Plan swept across the state. In 1834, the Whig Party, led by Murphey's acolytes, gained momentum in Washington and in Raleigh. The Whigs were able to unite forces with the West and some from the East with a platform calling for public schools, sound currency and banks, internal improvements, and shrewdly, constitutional reform, an issue that cut across party lines. The new constitution, approved in 1835, was a step forward in democratic government, although it stripped the vote from freed slaves and Native Americans, thus catering to prejudices at opposite ends of the political spectrum. Under the new constitution, "Christian" was substituted for "Protestant," thereby allowing Catholics, but not Jews or atheists, to run for public office. The property qualification for voting for North Carolina Senate candidates was reduced to fifty acres, but all tax-paying white males could vote for House members. And, though it had been hoped that the new constitution might erode sectionalism, it in fact revealed just how divided the state was when fewer than 2,500 Easterners voted in favor.

The Whig Party controlled the state from 1835 to 1850, although it was strongly opposed by the Democratic Party, particularly in the East. The Whigs were, for the time, quite modern, emphasizing roads, bridges, dams and public education – in many ways the old Murphey program. Its primary support came from businessmen and small farmers in the Piedmont and west who focused on developments that would have economic benefits. Its leaders were educated, had resources, and often were from old families who saw railroads and manufacturing as the wave of the future.

It was during the Whig ascendency that the Wilmington to Weldon Railroad was completed, giving North Carolina in 1840 the longest railroad in the world. The Democrats, on the other hand, were "standpatters" who essentially believed that the government was best when it governed least. In the Eastern part of the state they were the planter aristocracy, the slave holders who cared little about education, some of which might seep down to the slaves, or roads which might give slaves a route to freedom. These people were doing very well and had little interest in the problems of their fellow North Carolinians. Thus were planted the seeds of poverty and racism that haunt that part of the state today.

But the Whigs, after being entrenched in power for 15 years, had become complacent. And what happened to them and their power and direction is an example of one of the major recurring political patterns in North Carolina: efforts to move the state forward followed by periods of backsliding.

At a practical level, the Whigs didn't put forth the effort necessary to attract and train new leaders and began to lose public favor. The Democrats, on the other hand, were eager to regain power and were willing to adopt some of the modernizing Whig policies as their own. All, for instance, had begun to see the value of roads and railroads. So after regaining power in 1850, the Democrats pushed through legislation incorporating dozens of plank roads called "farmer's railroads." And in 1856 North Carolina eliminated property qualifications for voting, but it was the platform of the national Democratic Party that most helped the state party to overtake the more progressive Whigs. The Democrats were the party of the states' rights and pro-slavery policies. Although North Carolina was not as dependent on slave labor as many other southern states, states' rights was a popular issue for a majority of North Carolina's citizens, and that included the right of states to choose for themselves their laws on slavery. (This would not be the last time the race card was played at election time.)

With approach of the 1860 election, the Whigs, who had ceased to function as a party after the 1854 election, sprung into action. Instead of fighting the slavery issue head on, the Whigs, who now called themselves Republicans, shrewdly chose a closely linked tax issue as their cause. The wealthy slave owners benefitted from a tax system, which taxed slaves at a lower rate than other property. The Republicans argued that this was unfair, putting the middle class and the small landowner at a disadvantage. This strategy put the Democrats in the uncomfortable position of protecting the rich, who were a minority, and the status quo. Though it was by a narrow margin, the pro-slavery party, the Democrats, won. Not only had the voting swung back to the traditionalists, the results had revealed deep division in the state: many Democrats who voted for the pro-slavery candidate opposed secession. It was a clear instance of one step forward and two back, a pattern to be seen repeatedly from this time until the present. Also demonstrated was the narrow division between modernizers and traditionalists, another of those continuing patterns.

During the Period 1835 – 1860, the educated class, which identified primarily with the Whigs and then Democrats, had pulled the state forward, so instead of hanging their heads in shame, North Carolinians could take pride in their internal improvements: schools – especially the University of North Carolina in Chapel Hill – their railroads, their newspapers and other cultural improvements. Progress was relative to the previous Rip Van Winkle status; still, things had been getting better. But what happened at Fort Sumter would change all that.

THE WAR: FOLLOWING THE LEAD OF THE TRADITIONALISTS

The 1860 election had made clear that the state was badly divided on the issue of secession. While a strong majority favored slavery, leaving the Union was another matter entirely. Slowly and reluctantly dragged toward hostilities, North Carolina's participation was sealed when Lincoln called for troops from all states loyal to the Union. North Carolina was not willing to fight against the South. Then the president ordered the blockade of southern ports. At that point, even the Unionist newspaper editor William Woods Holden, who had started his political career as a Whig, called for secession. On May 20, 1861, North Carolina became the last southern state to leave the Union. It is interesting to wonder what might have happened had North Carolina not entered the war. The decision to secede and fight was one of the important turning points in the back-and-forth pattern of the state's modernization. Although few could see it at the time, the war would set the state backward, stopping all modernist movement and making race and any ideas that could be linked to the "Yankee government" even more divisive.

The differences within the state were briefly papered over with patriotic zeal. The history of North Carolina and the Civil War is truly a paradoxical one. As is widely known, North Carolina sent more troops into the Confederate Army than any state other than Virginia, and suffered between 33,000 and 35,000 casualties. Yet other thousands from North Carolina fought and died for the Union, and southern recruiters were roughly handled in the western counties. There was little military action within the borders, but North Carolinians were heavily involved in most of the major battles. It didn't take long before the former Unionists in the state began to have their worst fears realized – the dreams of an early Union victory quickly faded. In 1862 Zebulon Vance, a former Whig who served bravely in Lee's army, was called home, where he ran successfully for governor. Vance was a torn man; originally he hadn't favored secession, but he had joined the army of the Confederacy; he fought for the "cause" but he opposed many of the Confederate government's impositions on the state. It was ironic that the Confederacy, which had opposed federal interference in state affairs, had no qualms about making calls upon states for men, supplies and taxes. Vance was a states' rights man and he resisted Jefferson Davis just as he had resisted Lincoln.

As the casualties at Gettysburg and Vicksburg were made public, those with doubts about North Carolina's course had become more outspoken. William Woods Holden had had enough; he helped organize peace meetings in forty counties and his newspaper became an advocate of peace and even secession from the Confederacy. Vance, whose policy was, "fight the Yankees and fuss with the Confederacy," ran against Holden in the 1864 gubernatorial race, soundly defeating him.

As though it had been ordained, six months after the vote was counted, Sherman and his avenging army crossed the border into North Carolina. Surprisingly for such an agricultural state, North Carolina was home to the last remaining Confederate arsenal, located in Fayetteville. It was that which drew Sherman's attention and he burned the arsenal to the ground. Then his army swept north and east destroying almost everything of value in his path. A retreating southern army tried in vain to slow his advance at Averasboro and stop him at Bentonville, but after sparing the capital city Sherman moved on to Durham, where he dictated the terms of the peace Holden had sought. Although Appomattox is much celebrated, the real final peace of the war was signed in Durham, North Carolina.

The state had paid a terrible price in the war. Men had died on the battlefield, but life at home was hard as well. Even before Sherman's army destroyed railroads, factories, bridges, churches, and schools, carrying away livestock and valuables, there had been widespread deprivation among the populace. Farm fields were left untended while transportation systems withered. People went hungry, with almost half the population dependent on government handouts. And, with emancipation of slaves, $200 million worth of "human capital" was wiped out. Now, those 350,000 slaves were free to walk away from the fields and small businesses for which they had provided forced labor.

What was the lesson? North Carolina's citizens had been badly let down by their leaders. It was the planter aristocracy, abetted by some middle-class slave owners, who had led the secessionist wing of the Democratic Party. These were the same people who had opposed the modernizing impulse to invest in civic improvements in the years before the war. They were anti-government, anti-tax, anti-public schools, anti-social welfare – in short, they opposed change. Racism had given them an emotional appeal which attracted the laboring class and the small farmer, and these were the ones who bore the brunt of the war. The phrase, "a rich man's war and a poor man's fight" applied pointedly to the Old North State. Now the question was who would be chosen to lead the state out of its misery?

RECONSTRUCTION: A FAILED MODERNIST EXPERIMENT

At first the choice of who would lead was dictated by the federal government. Between 1865 and 1877, North Carolina suffered the indignity of a small but dwindling occupation by federal troops. Those 12 years are what are usually called "Reconstruction," but in North Carolina it only actually lasted from 1865 to 1870. With Lincoln dead, the Radical Republicans controlled Congress; their attitude: we won the war and now we're going to dictate the peace, including equal treatment and voting rights for blacks. Many in North Carolina saw this as federal overreach and reacted with ill-disguised resentment. Initially there was little they could do, as the provisional government appointed William Woods Holden governor until an election could be held.

But when that election was over, Holden was out and the traditionalist William Alexander Graham was in. This and other actions inspired the ire of Radical Republicans in Congress who saw North Carolina as trying to nullify the results of the war. Under the Radicals' direction, North and South Carolina were put under the direction of Union generals Dan Sickles and Edward Canby, who would oversee a convention intended to restore the states to the Union. In response, a North Carolina Republican Party was organized to help write a new constitution. In a bad political miscalculation for the traditionalists, many members of the old Democratic Party boycotted the Constitutional Convention. The result was a convention dominated by Republicans, many of whom were formerly Whigs, but including African Americans and some out-of-state representatives. The 1868 Constitution, not surprisingly, endorsed all the provisions desired by Washington — including the universal right to male suffrage — thereby immediately inspiring the opposition of white traditionalists. To be sure, they had some legitimate objections. Why should the state accept a constitution written by old Whigs or "Scalawags" as they were called, people from out of state, "carpetbaggers" and inexperienced African Americans? Moreover, it included provisions forced on them by the hated Yankees. Despite the fact that it was a modern constitution, to the traditionalists it seemed that never in the history had such an indignity occurred; it was, and remained a bitter pill for a poor but proud state. The Reconstruction experience actually planted the seeds that would set the course backward; the attempt to integrate loosed the forces of racism, which had economic as well as social roots.

In the election that followed, which included African American voters, it was not surprising that the Unionist, William Woods Holden, won the governorship. General Edward Canby, the military commander of the Second District, turned power over to the legislature, which quickly ratified the new constitution and elected representatives to Congress. On July 28, 1868, after ratifying the 14th Amendment, a Republican-dominated North Carolina was readmitted to the Union, but 73,000 people had voted against Holden, whom they saw as leading a coalition of traitors, African Americans and non-native troublemakers. Of course, they had a cadre of troublemakers of their own, including the Ku Klux Klan (KKK).

The Klan in North Carolina, as elsewhere in the South, never accepted the extension of rights to African Americans. There were cross burnings, lynchings and other efforts to keep Negroes "in their place." In response, the federal government passed the "Force Acts," or Civil Rights Acts of 1870 and 1871, in an attempt to protect the civil rights of Negro citizens.

This Klan organization was particularly effective when the elections of 1870 rolled around. By intimidating Negro voters, they greatly assisted the Democrats, who accused Governor Holden of corruption and capricious use of power. And to be sure, there was corruption to be found; Holden was so incensed by Democratic opposition that he sometimes used his power unwisely. All of this led to a Democratic victory, in which they won the majority of congressional seats and control of the legislature. Acting quickly, in December they moved to impeach Holden. This was accomplished in March of 1871. Holden was one of only two governors impeached in American history (he was pardoned posthumously in 2011).

The traditionalists, who had helped bring on the war and its attendant destruction, were back in power and Reconstruction was effectively over. It took six more years to complete "redemption" of the state, as the national Republican Party grew weary of trying to control the more reactionary policies of southern legislatures. In 1876 elections, Zebulon Vance, "the war governor" won a hotly contested election — but by only 14,000 votes — over his Republican opponent. In the run up to that election, some estimate that more than 100 blacks were killed in an effort to suppress their voting. Vance, who had conflicting emotions about secession and the role of government, was now a solid Democratic traditionalist and as fully intent as anyone on restoring white supremacy. He was to be assisted, perhaps unintentionally, by the newly elected President Rutherford B. Hayes, a Civil War veteran, who withdrew the last troops from the South in 1877, thus officially ending Reconstruction.

Though often misguided and over-zealous, the Reconstructionists, under the guise of the Republican Party, had tried, like the old Whigs, to bring North Carolina more in line with national norms. It was a "noble experiment," but it failed. To their peril they had added Negro rights to their old agenda of education, civic improvements and care for the less fortunate. Race relations were clearly the third rail of North Carolina politics and Holden and his supporters were not helped by the national Republican Party's outspoken advocacy of civil rights. But now the war was over and Reconstruction had failed — what would become of the modernist impulse in North Carolina?

CHAPTER II
"BACK TO THE PAST" 1876 - 1898

With Vance as governor and full control of the legislature, the Democrats set out to rule North Carolina. Although still a distinctly rural state (2 percent of the population lived in urban areas), the industrial revolution began to change the face of the state. Since the middle of the 19th century there had been some small, isolated manufacturing operations, notably in the Piedmont. But now with labor freed up from the farm, and money and manpower coming from the North (carpetbaggers), conditions were ripe for a manufacturing renaissance. Some of those carpetbaggers had operated textile mills in New England and saw the opportunity to take advantage of the abundance of waterpower and low-wage labor in the South. And the political clout of North Carolina business people would soon become one of the state's recurring themes.

INDUSTRIALIZATION AND JAMES B. DUKE

Textiles were among the first to catch on. North Carolina had always had an abundance of cotton, and by harnessing water power to turn the looms, there was the basis for a textile industry. Moreover, women and children could handle most of the labor and they didn't cost much, thereby contributing to the profit margin. Tightly controlled by a small number of families, the industry fed popular enthusiasm about a prospering North Carolina. Josephus Daniels and his Raleigh *News and Observer* (*N&O*) became a cheerleader for industrialization, seeing it as a vital component of a New South State. People were urged to, "Demand all legislative encouragement for manufacturing that may be consistent with true political economy." (*N&O* Nov. 9, 1880) The N&O saw manufacturing in company with the traditional agricultural base as a route to economic prosperity, which in turn could fund educational improvement. Daniels, despite the conservatism of his racial policies, was a strong supporter of public education; but, of course, separate but equal education.

Manufacturing in the state grew. For example, in 1865 Durham had one tobacco factory; by 1874 it had twelve; in 1880 the state boasted 126. The Duke family, enthusiastic capitalists, soon realized that by organizing tobacco farms to feed their factories and buying tobacco stores, they could control tobacco prices and maximize profit. They coupled this with a vigorous advertising campaign, which included giving away coupons that could be exchanged for prizes. Originally they produced plug, or chewing tobacco, but they diversified by adding cigarettes and pipe tobacco, soon monopolizing, through a trust, the whole industry. Using cutthroat business practices, the Dukes and a few others formed the American Tobacco Company, which in 1904 was valued at $294 million and controlled three quarters of the industry. The work force was made up primarily of Negroes and white young women whose annual wage was $136. That was $33 less than the textile workers and among the lowest wages in the country (Durden, *The Dukes of Durham*).

The new captains of industry settled in the growing towns in the middle part of the state. It was a time when material success was thought of as an indication of God's blessing. Social Darwinism or laissez faire capitalism – survival of the strongest – attracted a wide following. Moreover, it was thought, and by the newspapers encouraged, that these captains of industry were doing an immense public good by bringing North Carolina into the modern world. A mindset developed that equated industry, though totally private, as quasi-public enterprises. Lost in the enthusiasm was the fact that these industries were exploiting their workers — often poorly educated, and not infrequently women and children. With higher taxes, the wealth created could have been used to address educational and public service needs as well as make fortunes for the owners, but that was not the way it worked out. The captains of industry instead replaced the plantation aristocracy at the top of the social hierarchy and used their position to gain political leverage, which in turn protected their privileges and their low taxes. As it turned out, the "New South" movement, which championed industrialization and internal improvements, came with strings attached — low wages, no unions, low taxes and tepid support for public education.

Writing about the political leaders of this period, Walter Hines Page said, "...these men who ruled by the ghost called Public Opinion held the country and all the people back in almost the same economic and social state in which slavery had left them. There was no hope for the future under their domination... There would be no broadening of thought, because only old thoughts were acceptable; no change in society, because society's chief concern was to tolerate no change. The whole community would stand still, or slip further back." (Lefler, 513)

Using new technology, a rolling machine (and innovative sales techniques), W. Duke Sons and Company tobacco were able to out-produce and outsell their competitors. By cutting prices and buying retail outlets, Duke was able to diminish competition and force competitors to either sell out or go out of business. In 1890 James B. Duke brought the four remaining tobacco giants together as the American Tobacco Company. Within ten years American Tobacco virtually controlled the production and sale of cigarettes, plug, snuff and smoking tobacco. Duke had embraced the concept of the "holding" company, a trust that was a new type of monopoly.

American Tobacco was not the only monopoly growing out of the "Gilded Age" of unbridled capitalism – there was Standard Oil, among others. Seeing the potential for trusts or monopolies to stifle competition, Congress stepped in with the Sherman Antitrust Act. As the supporters of that act made clear, they did not mean to destroy the capitalist impulse, rather to regulate its most rapacious practices and thereby preserve competition in the public interest. It was beginning to dawn on people that capitalism needed to be regulated to protect it from itself. At the same time, some political movements were beginning to realize that farmers and laborers needed to be protected from businesses that were driven only by the profit motive. At the far left these political forces included communism or anarchism, while populism and progressivism were the more moderate examples. A radical stance was taken by the American Federation of Labor (AFL), which in 1894 called for nationalizing all major industries and financial institutions. In much of the country labor unions were striking for higher wages and better working conditions, but not in North Carolina, where businesses were protect by "right-to-work" laws.

Of the new manufacturing moguls, historian Holland Thompson said, "They are cold, shrewd, far-sighted. Sentiment in them does not interfere with the strict working of the privilege of self-advantage." Another noted, "Industry was so potent in state development that it became the beneficiary of the dominant Democratic Party." (Lefler, 513) Indeed, that party, which shared their values, was only too happy to cater to manufacturers' needs. The Democrats, as an article of faith, believed in the sanctity of private property. Consequently, they looked for other ways to advance, (read: make wealthy) their conservative patrons. It didn't take long to fasten on the railroads as a potential bonanza. Previous administrations had supported railroad construction by selling bonds. Through this method North Carolina had built a system of publicly owned small rail lines. Beginning in the 1870s North Carolina began to lease its railroads to northern interests for periods up to 99 years; in other words, they sold state property. This, in combination with favorable tax rates, led to a rapid expansion in rail mileage from 1,500 miles in 1880 to 3,381 in 1900. At the same time, smaller lines began to consolidate, until at the end of the century, there were only three main lines that were able to control rates and make a hefty profit.

THE FUSIONIST REACTION: A COALITION WINS THE DAY

Developments in industry didn't go unnoticed by the farming and laboring classes. Monopoly, whether in rails or tobacco, gave the owners control over wages and prices. Soon discontent started to grow, first among the farmers and then with labor. Not surprisingly, the Democrats in Raleigh did not believe in relieving these problems through tax policy. Indeed, they took a further step to protect the wealthy, devising a system that exempted their intangible personal property from tax and assessing their real property, including factories, at a low rate. Railroads enjoyed an even lower tax rate and, of course, there was no income tax. This seemed to the ruling party an enlightened policy, since the state was so lucky to have these wealth-creators in North Carolina pushing it forward. It was the 19th century version of trickle- down economics. Actually, many of these plutocrats weren't interested in pushing the state forward. Instead, they opposed the public education program, poorly funded as it was, partially on grounds that educated workers might demand higher pay or even unions. In their view, government should act on the principle of laissez faire, essentially staying out of the way of private industry. Of course, tax revenue had to come from somewhere and so farmers found themselves paying a disproportionate share.

The working class also had other grievances – low wages, unhealthy working conditions, long hours and unsafe practices in the factories and on the rail lines. The labor union movement was sweeping the country, but it never gained much traction in North Carolina because of the unified opposition of the "New South" businessmen. However, labor and the farmers began to see that they had common enemies in the corporations, trusts, railroads, the merchant class, banks and Wall Street. These sensitivities were heightened by the 1893 banking crisis and ensuing recession. It was the worst economic downturn since the Civil War and everyone, particularly the less fortunate, were looking for scapegoats. Since the Democrats were in power, nationally and at the state level, they made attractive targets.

There also was unhappiness about the neglect of public education, which had never recovered after the war. The University of North Carolina had reopened and there were educational opportunities for those who could send their children to private academies, but the mass of the public went uneducated. The Democrats were at best indifferent, or, in some cases, openly hostile, to public education. In 1890 the per capita school tax was 44-cents per year while the national average was $2.11. North Carolina was going back to sleep.

Whether it was the proverbial straw that broke the camel's back or not, the policy out of Raleigh that attacked local self-government certainly added to the list of grievances. The Democrats decided that they could best control the state by taking control of the counties. This was accomplished by vesting the power to appoint county commissioners in the hands of the justice of the peace, who was appointed by the General Assembly. A neat trick to be sure, but this policy was sure to incense the more "democratic" of the Democrats, as well as the Republicans.

Change was coming. Raleigh had been ruled by Democrats for 17 years; but finally the farmers, inspired by the Populist Party, the workers, and the Republicans, who had remained strong throughout the period, "fused" with the liberal Democrats and threw the rascals out in the 1894 election. The lesson was plain to see. If an entrenched party, in this case the Democrats, were to be ousted it would have to be by a coalition. It was the Populists, often rural, often poor, who because of economic grievances this time turned the tide. The Populists were no less racist than anyone else, but in 1894 their pocketbooks trumped their prejudices. They would return to the Democratic fold in 1898 and then again in the mid-20th century to help determine policy.

The Fusionists, as they were called, were an amalgamation of political interest groups. Their program sought to put North Carolina back on a competitive path toward more generally shared prosperity. Their reforms included giving more power back to the counties and putting more money into public education and into the state university and teacher education schools, all of which were to be funded by moderately higher taxes. The increase in government expenditures stirred strong Democratic opposition. It paled, however, in comparison to the backlash against the Fusionist efforts to include more Negroes in office and appointed positions. There never were large numbers of African American office holders; those who did hold public office were mostly limited to the eastern counties where African Americans made up to 50 percent or more of the population. This policy of African American inclusion was not popular with many of the farmers of the Populist persuasion and would be the undoing of the Fusionists. The

Democrats and the KKK succeeded in bringing race, always a sensitive issue, to the forefront.

The election of 1896 was a hotly contested and confusing one. At the national level, the Democrats ran William J. Bryan, who was a reformer and the farmers' friend. The Republicans ran William McKinley, who was philosophically conservative and specifically a supporter of big business. Many of the Populists broke ranks and voted for Bryan, with some returning to the Democratic candidates for statewide office. When the dust cleared, the Fusionists were still in control of the legislature and the governor's office, filled by Daniel Russell, whose family had been prominent Whigs. He had fought for the Confederacy even though he was a Unionist. After the war, he joined the Republican Party and then, in 1894, the Fusionists. Unfortunately for the Fusionists, they had been helped over the finish line by a growing African American vote. Although Russell's administration further increased the appropriations for public education and tried to take back some of the railroad property sold by previous administrations, it was the African American race issue that provided fodder for the Democratic challenge and broke the power of the Republican/Populist alliance.

1898

Josephus Daniels of the Raleigh *N&O* did everything possible to fuel the fire over the next election in 1898. It was a full-blown racist campaign. Daniels viewed Wilmington as a Fusionist stronghold complete with African American inclusion. The African American was pictured in his newspaper as the beast who was feasting on the flesh of innocent southern womanhood. The underlying message was that the Negro was an ignorant tool in the hands of Fusion politicians who sought to overturn "white supremacy." (Craig, *Josephus Daniels*)

The brains behind the campaign were archconservative political organizer Funifold Simmons, who would create the so-called Simmons Dynasty, and Charles B. Aycock, newspaperman, lawyer, failed candidate for the U.S. House and later governor. Both were effective race-baiters. They led emotional rallies and used the KKK and the Red Shirts, armed gangs of white terrorists, to intimidate voters. There were others as well who found it advantageous to support the Democrats. The press, particularly the *Raleigh N&O*, poured fuel on the fire by featuring dramatic accounts of Negros disturbing the peace and otherwise ignoring the law. Although Daniels no doubt harbored racist sentiments, the drama was also good for sales. Pulitzer and Hearst had used similar tactics to promote the Spanish American War. Business owners were assured by Democratic spokespeople that under their leadership, taxes would not be raised and that the state would not increase the funding for institutions of higher learning. When the votes were counted, it appeared that race baiting and appeals to the oligarchs of industry paid off: the Democrats won 134 seats in the General Assembly to thirty for the Republicans.

In Wilmington, then the state's largest city and one with a majority African American population, victory in the election was not enough. There were still Fusionist officials in office – and the well-paid customs collector was African American. That could be solved quickly by mob violence. Whites staged a coup, running elected officials out of office, burning a black newspaper building, firing on blacks in the street and killing at least 25. Appeals for federal assistance from Republican President William McKinley went unanswered. It was another signal that the South was now free to set its own course. Negro property owners fled town, while those who remained learned a lesson about "the New South": keep your head down. (Umfleet, *A Day of Blood: The 1898 Wilmington Race Riot*)

In four brief years, North Carolina had gone from a state making some progress materially and socially to a state turning back the calendar.

One area where the state had not made progress was in education. The University of North Carolina, which had reopened in 1875, had no state appropriations until 1881. It had low enrollment and had yet to capture the public imagination. Many of the wealthier class chose to send their children to the church-related schools, particularly those run by Baptists, Methodists and Presbyterians. One of the complaints against the state university was that its curriculum put heavy emphasis on the classics, while some prominent individuals sought a more practical education. As General D. H. Hill said, "The old plan of education in the balmy days of the South gave us orators and statesmen, but did nothing to enrich us, nothing to promote material greatness..." It was this attitude and the federal support for land-grant colleges, which led in 1889 to the opening of the state Agricultural and Mechanical College (North Carolina State University) as a rival to "the University" at Chapel Hill, which some saw as educating a group of intellectual elitists.

In 2013 Governor Pat McCrory gave an interview that, while not as eloquent as General Hill's, carried the same message. He said that an "educational elite" was dominating higher education, "offering courses that have no path to jobs." He said he would favor funding "not based on how many butts in seats, but how many of those butts can get jobs."

The public schools struggled during the last quarter of the 20th century. Although the law called for four months of school for all children, the General Assembly consistently violated the law by not making sufficient appropriations, in order to keep taxes low. By 1900 the public school system was actually "and relatively worse than it had been in 1860. It was perhaps the poorest in the U.S." (Lefler p. 536). There may have been other reasons, but as one historian puts it, "The real explanation for the state's loss of educational rank, even in the South, was a colossal general indifference to public education and a sterile, reactionary political leadership." Moreover, "the ignorant tax-voting masses were generally indifferent," while "some of the wealthy opposed the entire concept of public education and patronized the private schools." (Lefler, 536)

CHAPTER III
THE REDEEMERS COMETH

The original Redeemers, invoking a term from Christian theology, had helped end Reconstruction in the 1870s. The new Redeemers, who were Democrats, also called themselves White Supremacists, and swept back into power in 1898. ("The second Redemption" the Civil War era in North Carolina, History Department, North Carolina State University)

They wasted no time quickly passing laws that favored business interests, lowering taxes, suppressing voting and reducing local autonomy. But to deal with the "problem" of the Negro, they resorted to constitutional means. To get around the 15th Amendment to the U.S. Constitution, which granted African American men the right to vote, they rewrote their own Constitution. Their new version featured an amendment that became known as a "grandfather" clause. If you had voted or paid poll tax prior to 1867, you didn't have to pass a literacy test. Obviously no Negroes had voted prior to 1867, so they had to read or write or interpret any part of the Constitution a registrar chose in order to vote. For poor whites who didn't pass the 1867 requirement, they could register before 1908 and be enfranchised. The literacy tests they had to pass, before sympathetic registrars, were far simpler.

These policies were all part of the Redeemers "reform" package. Bring back the past, before the South was defeated by the Yankees, before businesses had to put up with troublesome regulations, before taxes were squandered on public schools, and very importantly, before "uppity Negros" had forgotten their place. Back to an imagined, magnolia-scented, better past.

This suffrage amendment to the Constitution had to be passed by public referendum prior to 1900. Many poor whites were worried about their voting rights along with many others who were offended by the chicanery and what it said about the state. To sweeten the pot, the Democrats promised modernist reforms like more funds for education and services for the poor. In their view, reforms were worth it if they could deny Republicans 50,000 potential Negro voters. Even Prohibition became mixed up in the disenfranchisement debate. The Republicans were viewed as the wets, who, among other things, plied Negroes with alcohol. By championing Prohibition, white Democrats and Populists believed that "to forbid the sale of legal liquor, and so presumably drive up the price of the bootleg product, would be to deprive (African Americans) of alcohol... so make it easier to keep ([them] in their place)." This argument "was much used in winning over the vote of hard drinking poor whites." (Craig, 199) It also was used to pass Prohibition in 1908, twelve years before it became U.S. law.

The amendment passed, and with it two-party government in North Carolina. Between 1900 and 1920 the Republicans, who numbered at least a third of the population, succeeded in electing no governor, no state officer, no U.S. senator and only three members of the U.S. House. In the North Carolina Senate there were never more than four members who were Republican, and they were totally without power. The man calling the shots for the Democratic Party was Furnifold Simmons; his deep-rooted political machine made sure their candidates for governor and the U.S. Senate were elected. This was the Simmons Dynasty that held power from 1900 until 1930. During this period, the Democrats were responsible for what happened in North Carolina for good or ill.

In 1901 William McKinley was assassinated. McKinley had been one of Big Businesses' best friends, intellectually endorsing a policy of low regulation, laissez faire, and unfettered capitalism.

When Vice President Teddy Roosevelt succeed McKinley, he realized that only the federal government could regulate the activities of some of the "Captains of Industry" like John D. Rockefeller, J. P. Morgan and James

B. Duke. Roosevelt called them "malefactors of great wealth," and acted to protect the public from some of their most monopolistic practices.

Theodore Roosevelt was a strong supporter of the capitalist system and a thoroughly patriotic American, but he sensed there was something deeply wrong with our political and economic system. On August 31, 1910, at Osawatomie, Kansas, he gave one of the most important speeches in American history. It is known as the "New Nationalism" speech. In it he proposed that a strong federal government was essential to provide, "equality of opportunity" in the face of entrenched wealth. He quoted Abraham Lincoln, who had said, "Labor is prior to, and independent of capital. Capital is only the fruit of labor, and could never have existed if labor had not first existed. Labor is the superior of capital, and deserves much the higher consideration." Lincoln continued, "Property is the fruit of labor." Roosevelt observed, "In every wise struggle for the betterment one of the main objectives... has been to achieve in large measure a quality of opportunity."

He then cited one of the challenges to the equality of opportunity. "At many stages in the advance of humanity, the conflict between the men who possess more than they have earned and the men who have earned more than they possess is the central condition of progress. In our day it appears as the struggle of free men to gain and hold the right of self government as against the special interests who twist the methods of free government into machinery for defeating popular will." To protect the average citizen he suggested that our government — national and state — must be freed from the sinister influence or control of special interests... the Constitution guarantees protection to property and we must make the promise good, but it doesn't give the right of suffrage to any corporation...There can be no effective control of corporations while their political activities remain. To put an end to it will be anything but a short or easy task, but it can be done." Lest anyone miss his meaning, he went on to say, "The absence of effective State, and, especially national, restraint upon unfair money-getting has tended to create a small class of enormously wealthy and economically powerful men, whose chief objective is to hold and increase their power." (In

December 2011 President Barack Obama went to Osawatomie, Kansas, and reiterated his dedication to finding "equality of opportunity.")

But it was Teddy Roosevelt's successor, William Howard Taft, who decided to "break" the American tobacco trust. The litigation ended in 1911 when Duke was ordered by the Supreme Court to take apart the tobacco empire he had so elaborately put together. It was quite a blow, but Duke turned his energies and talents to building the Duke Power Company, among other enterprises. Headquartered in Charlotte, Duke Power grew over the years until, by 2013, it had become the largest electric power holding company in the U.S.

Woodrow Wilson was elected president in 1912. A self-described "progressive," he combined the policies of Roosevelt and Taft regarding big business: regulating where possible, breaking where necessary. During his administration the Clayton Antitrust Act (1914) was passed, which further restricted monopolies, granted workers' rights and established the Federal Trade Commission to stop unfair practices. He established the Federal Reserve System to help control banking practices, and instituted the graduated income tax to help balance the distribution of wealth.

THE GRAND BARGAIN

One historian sees these various actions by Teddy Roosevelt, Taft and Wilson – two Republicans and one Democrat – as laying the groundwork for a "grand bargain" (Keyssar, "The Real Grand Bargain"). Under this bargain, although never codified, capitalism would be allowed to endure, but only if it were subject to strict regulation and with a social safety net to protect citizens "against the shortcomings of a market economy." Moreover, workers were granted the right "to form unions and engage in collective bargaining." Finally, and this didn't come until the next Roosevelt was president, there would be more legislation.

The initial steps, Sherman Antitrust (1890), Pure Food and Drug (1905), busting American tobacco (1907-1911), establishing the Federal Reserve, and the graduated income tax were taken at a time when it wasn't at all clear that capitalism would survive. Between 1880 and 1920 hundreds of Socialists were elected to office, and there regularly was a Socialist candidate for president. In the 1912 presidential election, 75 percent of the vote went to candidates who declared themselves Socialists or Progressives.

The North Carolina Democratic Party would change with time. Over the years there was a slow modulating tendency toward a more modernist agenda. This may have been due in part to the influence of the national Democratic Party. Woodrow Wilson, elected in 1912, had spent part of his childhood in North Carolina and had many supporters in the state. Prominent among them was Josephus Daniels – yes, the same one who had used the Raleigh News and Observer to race-bait in 1898 – who became Secretary of the Navy. Wilson also was dependent on North Carolina in Congress. Senator Simmons, a racist and the boss of the state Democratic machine, was chairman of the Senate Finance Committee. Claude Kitchin was Democratic Leader of the House. Wilson was tolerant of the racial attitudes of these men, in part because he, himself, was no modernist on racial issues; moreover, he needed their votes for his progressive agenda of support for small businessmen and farmers; trust-busting to break up business monopolies; and advocacy for labor unions. North Carolina had voted for Wilson in 1912 and did so again in 1916, an indication of party discipline and a clear strategy of avoiding the race issue, while at the same time the president won support for his progressive policies from liberal Democrats within the state.

Starting in 1900, North Carolina Democrats became advocates for more state support for education and public services. In his 1901 inaugural address, Governor Aycock, the same man who had been so influential and racist in the 1898 campaign, said, "I pledged to the State, in its strength, its heart, its wealth to universal education. I promised the poor man, bound to a life of toil and struggle and poverty that life should be better for his boy and girl than it had been for him and his parents…" In fulfilling this pledge, money was poured into public schools; between 1900 and 1910, some 3,000 segregated public schools for whites as well as African Americans were established. It was Aycock's view that the Negro should learn "once and for all that there is unending separation of the races, that the two peoples may develop side-by-side to the fullest, but they cannot intermingle." (Daniels, *Editor in Politics*, 469) That obviously meant segregation now and segregation forever. (Aycock, once regarded by the Democratic Party as an icon, has become an embarrassment, as his racist sentiments have been revealed.)

Historian V. O. Key dates the modern era in North Carolina from the administration of Governor Aycock (1901-1905), which is ironic, given the positions Aycock held on race. It was Aycock's conviction that "the best investment a state can make is in the education of its children." In Key's view, from education "springs... the spirit of self examination that still sets North Carolina apart in the South." This being the case, Aycock deserves credit for laying the groundwork for a modern public education system. In 1918 a six-month school year became mandatory. By that time the appropriation for the University of North Carolina had gone from $155,000 to $2 million per year.

In 1917 North Carolina followed Woodrow Wilson into World War I, which brought further modernization and prosperity. The war was popular in the state, or at least it was strongly supported. Approximately 60,000 whites and more than 20,000 Negroes served in the armed forces. Our losses in the war were low – only 629 killed in action – with more dying of disease (1,542). North Carolina troops saw action as parts of two divisions, the Thirtieth "Old Hickory" Division and the First "Wildcat" Division. The war lasted for the United States only 18 months, but that was long enough to stir up patriotic sentiment, raise money for war bonds, and set our textile factories humming. North Carolina pine was needed to build the barracks at recently created military bases. There were training camps established in Charlotte, Raleigh, and Ft. Bragg near Fayetteville. Thousands of young men got their first taste of the South in these camps and gave North Carolinians some experience with Yankees who weren't an invading force. Remember, it had been only 53 years since the end of the Civil War and 41 years since the last federal troops had left the state. All in all, World War I was a positive experience for North Carolina, bringing more prosperity and exposure to new ideas.

Funds were available for educational improvements because the first two decades of the 20th century were prosperous ones for North Carolina, as they were for the nation as a whole. Increased electrical power, much of it developed by James B. Duke in the area between Durham and Charlotte, helped drive the rise in manufacturing. Textiles, tobacco and furniture were the leading industries, and their growth contributed to making North Carolina the leading manufacturing state in the Southeast. Factory output now far exceeded agricultural income, though the state remained a land of a few medium-sized cities and mosty small farms where life was hard, illiteracy was high and wages were low. The per capita income in North Carolina in 1929 was $328 per annum, which ranked it 44th out of 48 in the nation. "Thank God for Mississippi" was a common refrain.

The 1920s were a roller-coaster ride for North Carolinians, ending with a new awareness in the state that the federal government was not necessarily an enemy, but could be a force for growth and broader prosperity. Archibald Murphey had tried to drive home that theme a century earlier, but this time there would be practical application. New prosperity, which marked most of the decade for the country, was very evident in the state, although something short of roaring. The new money made possible improvements in infrastructure and schools, while at the same time fueling public optimism. But the state's basic fundamentalism, both at the social and religious level, was still much in evidence. In the 20s, one form this took was Christian fundamentalists disputing the science of evolution, campaigning against the teaching of it in public schools. Indeed they were intent on having creationism taught instead of evolution. And, after all, North Carolina had become a leader in the nation when it had enacted Prohibition in 1908.

Not surprisingly, many North Carolinians fell in step with nativism — giving certain established groups privileges not accorded to newer arrivals — and with the "Red Scare," which built on the fear that Communists or Socialists were threatening American values and our freedoms. A patriotism movement swept the state, sometimes focusing on the feeble labor unions as un-American. A revived KKK took up the cause, and although not as powerful as during Reconstruction or the 1898 period, they continued to intimidate Negroes and others whom they saw as threats to the existing order. Usually the Klansmen were working class or farming people who perpetuated the image of the ignorant, bigoted North Carolina "redneck," but they had the behind-the-scenes support of business owners and others who had an interest in keeping wages low and potential dissidents in their place.

An example of the cover given these elements was Lee Overman, North Carolina's first popularly elected senator (prior to progressive reforms, senators had been appointed). Overman chaired a committee investigating un-American activities during the Red Scare. Later he helped lead a filibuster against a federal anti-lynching bill —- which he contended would encourage ignorant black people in the South to "commit the foulest outrages;" read, rape. Southern senators continued to oppose the anti-lynching laws well into the 1950s despite passage in the House and entreaties by various presidents.

The 19th Amendment to the U.S. Constitution, giving women the right to vote, had tough sledding in North Carolina. In August of 1920 a document was sent from Raleigh to the Tennessee General Assembly urging that body not to ratify the amendment. The document sent from the North Carolina House of Representatives stated that the signers represent a majority of House members who would not vote for the "Susan B. Anthony Amendment" (sounds like Obamacare). Their opposition was based on the proposition that such an amendment would interfere with the "sovereignty" of the states. In other words, it was another example of attempted usurpation of states' rights by the federal government. And in North Carolina, states' rights trumped citizens' rights to vote. North Carolina was true to its promise and did not vote to ratify the "Susan B. Anthony Amendment," but was forced to comply when Tennessee and enough other states did so, making it law. It was not until 1971 that North Carolina's legislature ratified the 19th Amendment. In this case voter suppression hadn't worked.

The rights of Native Americans to vote is a longer, more convoluted story of voter suppression. In 1920 both Native American (and here I refer to the Eastern Band of Cherokee) men and women showed up to vote. When the votes were counted in Jackson County, Republicans won nearly every race by a narrow margin. "Foul," claimed the Democrats who were running the state, who threw out the Native American vote on the grounds that they weren't citizens. Congress responded in 1924 by passing the Indian Citizenship Act, conferring citizenship on all Native Americans. This was not good enough for the North Carolina attorney general, who continued to insist that the state's Native Americans weren't covered. Congress, therefore, passed another act in 1929 specifically referencing the Eastern Band.

That still failed to change the attitude of North Carolina voter registrars. In 1937 the solicitor general found that North Carolina was claiming Native Americans couldn't vote because they were illiterate. In 1940 Congress passed the Nationality Act again, confirming Native American citizenship, perhaps as a justification for asking them to register for the draft. The Eastern Cherokee Tribal Council protested, asserting that their treatment in regards to voting made them suspect they might not be treated fairly by draft boards. The council stated that, "any organization or group that would deprive a people of as sacred a right as the right of suffrage would not hesitate to deprive them of other constitutional rights including the three inalienable rights – life, liberty, and the pursuit of happiness, if the opportunity to do so presented itself." But register they did, and then 300 Native Americans from North Carolina served in the military during World War II.

But despite the racism and voter suppression that marked the state during this period, it was also a time when the first green shoots of a modern North Carolina began to poke through our fertile soil. Good schools and roads were beginning to be seen as good for business. Governor Cameron Morrison took office in 1921 and immediately set about improving the state's road system, which was in woeful condition. Though his political roots and many of his positions, including opposition to women's suffrage, were traditionalist, he made some important modernist moves. He significantly increased the funding for Chapel Hill and other state institutions of higher learning. This he justified on grounds that education spending was an investment in the state's future. An educated workforce and good schools would attract more business enterprises looking for a good quality of life and capable workers. Nor were the public schools neglected. Special building funds were made available to the counties while teacher salaries were increased — an idea that seems to have lost appeal for the state government of 2010 — along with a more rigorous set of requirements for certification.

The popularity of Morrison and his "business progressivism" indicated that more and more North Carolinians were coming to see government as a source for public good. "By the 1920s the broad modern social concept of government as a service agency for community development had triumphed." (Lefler, 603) All this was costly, of course, and when the new governor, Angus McLean, took over in 1925 the state debt was almost $114 million, the highest per capita in the nation. McLean put the brakes on state spending, but didn't overturn Morrison's modernist moves.

North Carolina voters broke from the national Democratic ranks in the 1928 election when they voted for Herbert Hoover. The Democratic candidate was Al Smith, the Governor of New York, whom Senator Furnifold Simmons characterized as an urban elitist who drank and bowed down to the Pope. Smith's opposition to Prohibition and his Catholicism was too much for the 350,000 North Carolinians who followed Simmons' lead. The Democrats, however, held on to the most state offices and the governorship. On a positive note, however, the 1928 election spelled the end of the white supremacist Simmons machine. Simmons lost power and his Senate seat in large part because he had opposed his party's candidate for president. White supremacy attitudes in the state did not die, but that movement lost some of its organized power.

A CRACK IN THE TRADITIONAL FAÇADE

It was the fate of Governor O. Max Gardner to take the state through the early years of the Great Depression. Gardner, a mill owner, realized that something dramatic needed to be done as the bottom dropped out, first for agricultural products and then for manufactured goods. He responded by consolidating state government functions and reducing the tax burden on individuals. Business wanted to see corporate taxes reduced as well, but in a reversal for a Democratic regime, Gardner oversaw an increase in corporate taxes, figuring that business could more easily live with an increase than the public could with a regressive sales tax. All in all, Gardner was a modern governor doing things like calling on the Brookings Institution for help in reorganizing state government. He instituted tax reform, led the state in reorganizing the university system, became the "father" of the state-supported public schools, championed health programs and improved our public infrastructure. Not bad in a state staggered by the Depression. Not incidentally, he, like Simmons, built a political machine to perpetuate his legacy.

GARDNER'S SHELBY DYNASTY

Gardner's "Shelby Dynasty"— Gardner was from Shelby, just west of Charlotte — would run the state into the 1950s. Throughout this period it was never doubted that "the ultimate political power of the state represented large business and financial interests." Some governors were more forward-looking than others, but in basic ways they were the same. As V. O. Key wrote about North Carolina governors, "Progressive, forward-looking, yes, but always sound, always the kind of government liked by the big investor, the big employer." Those business interests were always willing to "be fair," but not at the expense of their interests. These attitudes insured that "a sympathetic respect for the problems of corporate capital and of the large employers permeates the state's politics and government. For half a century an economic oligarchy held sway." (Key, 211-214) And while this policy was good for the oligarchy, the average North Carolinian remained poor and poorly schooled.

The year 1932 brought Franklin Delano Roosevelt into the White House and into the hearts of many North Carolinians, who welcomed and benefitted from many of his reforms. Roosevelt's administration was the first Democratic one in 12 years, and his vision meshed with that of those people who had been hammered by the Depression. However, opposition to the New Deal was also strong, as the business interests saw him as promoting Socialism with programs that were distinctly un-American. But the "Grand Bargain" held and the New Deal years saw the Glass-Stegall Banking Act (1933), Social Security (1935), the National Labor Relations Act (1935), and the Rural Electrification Act (1935) that gave protection to labor organizers. Roosevelt was clearly progressive, even liberal, but historians debate whether he pursued the policies that he did out of conviction or whether he was really trying to save capitalism from a more radical takeover. (And I am one 20th century historian who believes that much of Franklin Roosevelt's motivation for the New Deal was to save market capitalism from itself. Remember, in the 1930s much of the world was dominated by Fascists, Communists or Socialists. Roosevelt avoided that fate by accepting the Grand Bargain.) Saint or demon, he appealed to the majority of North Carolinians and helped convince them that "government" cared about them. Government had seldom been seen this way before and the new attitude would pave the way for the more modernizing governors who came in the 1950s.

During this period the public wanted taxes cut, but Governor John C. B. Ehringhaus and others realized that further reducing government revenue would only put the state deeper in debt. A cry went up to cut allocations for schools and some wanted a luxury tax on the wealthy. For their part, the business community opposed all tax increases. The Governor had to walk a fine line, and he did, declaring that the priority had to be paying the school bonds. Even in the worst of times, in his view, education had to be protected, even if that meant a sales tax, which he did not want. Finally a balance was struck between revenue enhancement for schools and expenditure reduction. A 3 percent sales tax was levied and state services were reduced, while teacher and other state employees' salaries were cut.

Despite these cuts, Ehringhaus made a significant commitment to the public school system. In addition to the infusion of funds, the state also took over from the counties the primary responsibility for the schools. Also, the time of attendance was increased from six months to eight. It is interesting that the schools got this endorsement in hard economic times from a legislature led by elected officials from rural North Carolina. The explanation has to be that those legislators were beginning to see that change was coming in rural counties. The first sign was that women were leaving the farm to work in small cut-and-sew factories that dotted the state. Soon some of the men began working the farms only part time, spending other hours supplementing their income in the factories. The sense that agriculture was slowly giving way to manufacturing was beginning to seep down, and with it came recognition that farmers' children needed more education. For residents of rural North Carolina, public schools were their lifeline to a better future. While encouraging, this did not mean an overall change in attitude regarding social issues. Rural areas remained traditionalist on many matters and most certainly on the issue of race—maintaining two school systems, separate and unequal, was better than integration.

THE NEW DEAL

The new Deal would bring other changes to North Carolina. The Civilian Conservation Corp (CCC) and the Public Works Administration (PWA), both hallmarks of the New Deal, funneled money into North Carolina. The CCC employed 27,000 men between 1933 and 1935, who worked out of 66 camps, building trails, cutting fire roads in national forests and otherwise improving state property. With unemployment of at least 12 percent there were plenty of projects for the Works Projects Administration (WPA) and Federal Agency Relief Administration (FERA) to invest in, and thousands who needed direct relief. By 1935 these two federal programs had pumped $53 million into the state. In total the state received between 1933 and 1938 some $428 million in federal aid through a variety of "alphabet soup" agencies that did everything from paying social security, to farm subsidies, to building roads and bridges, to decorating public building and subsidizing the arts. Without this infusion of federal funds, seen by some as Soviet-style intrusion, it is hard to see how the state could have made it.

Loved by many—FDR won in 1936 and in 1940 by a margin of 60 percent over his opponents—he was still bitterly opposed by many in the business community. By them he was seen as interfering with the banks by way of the Glass-Steagall Act, which separated commercial banking from investment banking. (No more "gambling with other people's money," said the President.) He also interfered with the power companies, both by setting up a rate commission and getting directly into the electricity business via the Tennessee Valley Authority (TVA), which provided power at low rates to parts of Western North Carolina. Other projects were seen by some as "boondoggles" and a waste of public funds; and while they may have been, they put spending money in the people's pockets. Through these programs and those at the state level, North Carolina found itself at the end of the decade economically back where it had been in 1929. A lost decade to be sure, but through a combination of state and federal aid and innovation, the Old North State could look to the future battered but unbowed.

Part of the battering had been the Depression, though the traditionalist policies put in practice after 1898 had also helped drag the state down, or at least hold it back. After almost fifty years of traditional rule, North Carolina was marked by poverty, lack of good public education, and segregationist policies that kept African Americans disenfranchised. Although there had been some enlightened governors and moderate legislators, it would be hard to characterize the period as anything but a failure in terms of the public welfare.

WORLD WAR II

The Second World War opened the eyes of many North Carolinians to the wider world, thereby leading more people to favor modernization. One of the first effects, though, was a booming statewide economy. If the New Deal brought North Carolina a sustaining diet, World War II brought it a banquet. The textile mills saw production soar as the government contracted for everything from uniforms to blankets. The draft ended the unemployment problem, as did the increased demand in the tobacco and furniture factories. One sobering note was the number of young men rejected for service, reflecting the poor state of education, sanitation and public health within the state. Almost 30 percent of inductees from North Carolina were rejected versus a rate of less than 25 percent for the nation as a whole. But the training of soldiers brought business and work to the state; many of the men selected were trained at Fort Bragg in Fayetteville or Camp Lejeune in Jacksonville, with both towns growing dramatically. Ships were built in Wilmington, while other parts of Eastern North Carolina prospered as a result of bases in Elizabeth City, Edenton and Camps Davis and Butner. All in all 362,000 men and women served in the armed forces, which provided for many of them their first experience out of the state. Casualties were not as severe, proportionately, as they had been in the Civil War; still, between 7,000 and 8,000 were killed and many thousands more wounded. For many women, war work provided income and experience they had never had before, and prompted them to seek further advancement toward equality once the war was over. The same was true for African American servicemen, who came home expecting some reforms in recognition of their sacrifices.

In hindsight, the war was a formative experience for North Carolina. It was clear that the federal government could, and did, have a positive impact in the lives of people. While indeed war is a terrible thing, it does have some positive aspects. It ended the Great Depression, inflated the factory output, absorbed all the cotton and tobacco the state could grow, gave thousands an opportunity to see how other Americans lived, and gave thousands practical education learning to fly planes, drive trucks and other new skills. It also showed that North Carolina still needed to improve its education and public health system if it were to be truly competitive.

KERR SCOTT – THE HAW RIVER POPULIST

The prosperity created by the war put North Carolina in a position to go forward. The first post-war governor, Gregg Cherry, put an emphasis on public schools, public health and hospital construction. Salaries for public employees and teachers were raised, a four-year medical school at Chapel Hill was established, and a five-year hospital building plan was adopted. But it was Governor Kerr Scott (1949 – 1953) who boldly adopted a "Go Forward" policy for the state. As a farmer, Scott knew that local roads still needed improvement, so he supported a $200 million road bond issue to "get (farmers) out of the mud." He also encouraged the General Assembly to appropriate hundreds of millions of dollars for state agencies to build and repair buildings and make other improvements to better serve the state's citizens. It was also during his administration that the ports at Wilmington and Morehead City received construction and improvement funds.

A business-friendly populist, Scott could see that educational advancement, as well as the internal improvements, was in the economic interests of the state. Therefore, more funds were made available to the university system and North Carolina joined the Southern Regional Education Board (SREB), which was a consortium of southern states intended to develop regional educational services in technological and scientific areas. Scott also emphasized the public school system by raising teacher salaries, and he supported the rural electrification program and better public health and welfare. According to one historian, Kerr Scott had "created the modern progressive wing of the Democratic Party." Jim Hunt, who became governor 28 years later, would say that "Kerr Scott was our political savior." He was "giving us a whole new life by bringing us these opportunities." (Christensen, 153) Not since the Fusionists had there been this close an alliance between the old line Democrats and the rural populists. Scott did not seek to break the power of the oligarchs; rather he sought a way to find common ground. Once again an alliance breached strict party lines and brought forward movement.

THE GRAHAM-SMITH PRIMARY:
TRADITION TRUMPS PROGRESS

This period was the beginning of a post-war moderate/progressive push to put North Carolina in the forefront of southern states. Yet some aspects of the national Democratic Party's platform did not fit well with

North Carolinians' essential traditionalism, especially on the racial front. President Harry Truman had integrated the armed forces, and then in 1950 a federal court ordered the UNC Law School to admit qualified Negro applicants. This did not go down well with many citizens and they showed it during the senatorial primary between Dr. Frank Graham, the beloved liberal former president of the University of North Carolina and the racist Willis Smith. Graham had won the first primary with 303,000 to Smith's 250,000. Initially Smith was reluctant to ask for a runoff but his young publicity director, Jesse Helms, effectively used broadcast ads and fliers to urge him to run. Ultimately Smith agreed. Smith was, in the words of historian William Powell, a member of the "conservative 'plutocracy' that had governed North Carolina since 1930." (Powell, 1050) It was an ugly campaign, during which Jesse Helms, who would become dean of extreme conservatism in the state, first proved his effectiveness. Helms later downplayed his role, but there is good evidence that he was involved in the 1950 election up to his armpits — even taking scissors to crop photos to make Graham appear more Negro-friendly. Graham was smeared as a Communist who favored integration and "intermingling" of races. Smith won with 281,000 to Graham's 261,000 in an election which was, again, in the words of Powell, "a triumph of tradition over liberalism." One more time, as in 1898, race provided the impetus to turn North Carolina backward and provide a warning that despite a recent record of moderate modernism, there was still a deep strain of social conservatism. In addition it gave impetus to the career of Jesse Helms, who made his initial trip to Washington as Smith's administrative assistant.

With Graham defeated, attention turned to the gubernatorial race between William B. Umstead (D) versus H. F. "Chub" Seawell, Jr. (R). Many wondered whether the bitter Graham/Smith fight would split the Democratic Party, but the wound was taped over and Umstead won by 412,977 votes. That should not, however, be taken to mean that all the state's Democrats shared ideology. There were many traditional conservatives who stood far to the right to of the younger, more forward-looking party members.

Umstead died in office after only 16 months, to be replaced by Lt. Governor Luther Hodges. Hodges was the last governor in the "Shelby Dynasty" begun by O. Max Gardner. Hodges started in the textile industry as an ordinary mill worker and rose to the top. By the time he retired at the age of 52, he was overseeing Fieldcrest Mills in six states. A big man, Hodges had none of the back-slapping, story-telling demeanor of the average politician. He was used to issuing orders and being obeyed. But he was a moderate, or at least he preached moderation. Naturally he intended to protect North Carolina's industrialists against labor unions. Here he was simply maintaining the status quo — the state had the lowest percentage of unionized laborers in the country. But it didn't take long for Hodges to make the connection between North Carolina's non-unionized workers and low wages. He learned that in 1953 North Carolina ranked 44 out of 48 states in per capita income. It was also the case that North Carolina factory workers were the lowest paid in the country and the wages in textile mills were part of the problem. Whether he had known this as head of a textile conglomerate or not, as governor he decided that the state simply had to attract new kinds of industry — industries that would pay higher wages. Though he never said so, Hodges must have realized that after fifty years of traditionalist rule, his state had hardly moved the economic needle for most of his constituents.

Hodges' most lasting contribution to the solution was the development of the Research Triangle Park, which called upon the research capabilities of the faculties at Duke, Chapel Hill and N. C. State. Hodges put together a nonprofit corporation that purchased 4,000 acres of scrub pine land and recruited a board including leaders in business and academia to start an institution that would "create a more sustainable economic base that would carry North Carolina into the 21st century." Today there are more than 170 global companies located in the park. What Hodges demonstrated here was the use of facts or metrics to guide his policies; he looked at North Carolina's national ranking in wages and devised a way to bring in better jobs. This fact-based policy-making is the hallmark of the best of the modernizing governors, whereas traditionalists, including those of the second decade of the 21st century, are likely to make decisions based on ideology.

If Hodges needed any further reasons to see the connection between education and improving the economic well being of the state, he got it in 1955 from the report of the Bryant Committee on Higher Education. The report was scathing in its assessment of the state's institutions of higher learning and sought to bring more rationality to the UNC System. Victor Bryant noted that while the state could not afford "several great universities," it should "have at least one." This led to the elevation of Chapel Hill as the state's leading university, the formation of the Board of Higher Education, as well as the beginning of President William Friday's career as the broad-minded champion of higher education in North Carolina.

Although a good university prior to the 1950s, it was only as the state began to move forward that the university blossomed. Much of the credit goes to William Friday, president from 1956 to 1986. He was a master politician as well as a talented administrator who became something of a conscience for the state. He wooed the politicians and the business leaders, convincing them that the university would be an economic engine. Promoting University of North Carolina-Chapel Hill, North Carolina State, and Duke as research powerhouses, he won important adherents in Raleigh and the boardroom. People began to take pride in their institutions of higher learning as they watched the university advance in national ranking.

The issue that consumed most of Governor Hodges' time was integration of the state's public schools. Here Governor Hodges' "moderation" was much in evidence. Brown versus Board of Education, in which the Supreme Court ruled segregated schools unconstitutional, had been handed down while Umstead was still alive, but Hodges inherited the challenges that resulted from it. The governor, like most white North Carolinians, opposed the decision; yet he could see that violence or closing the schools would hurt North Carolina's image and make business recruiting, to which he was committed, much more difficult. Hodges responded by appointing a commission to study the problem and make recommendations, at the same time announcing, "The white citizens of the state will resist integration strenuously, resourcefully and with growing bitterness." When schools opened in August, he said his policy was to follow the lead of the General Assembly – which opposed integration – "but, at the same time avoid defiance or evasion of the opinion of the U.S. Supreme Court" by having white and black students <u>voluntarily</u> attend separate schools.

This was really walking a fine line. He was later given cover when the Pearsall Commission reported in the spring of 1956. Their proposal, adopted by an overwhelming popular vote in September, provided that parents could send their students to private schools at state expense if the local school board closed the public schools. This never happened and was later ruled unconstitutional; however, it gave Hodges political protection and he got national praise for his "moderate" handling of the issue. As one historian has noted: "To qualify as a moderate in the South of the 1950s, one just had to avoid being a rabid segregationist." (Pearce, 163)

One issue that couldn't be dodged was the integration of the university. In 1955, a federal court ordered that three black students should be admitted as undergraduates to Chapel Hill. They were peacefully admitted, thus integrating the first public university in the South. Standing in the school house door was not Hodges' style, nor was it a style that appealed to most North Carolinians. That should not be taken to mean that there was not a substantial number of North Carolinians who were willing to fight integration.

"Most businessmen, the evidence suggests, preferred segregation, and during the mid-fifties they for the most part took studious care not to become involved in the fray over schools," wrote historian Numan Bartley. "But the financiers, merchants, publishers and industrialists also had a substantial stake in economic growth and dreaded the impact of closed schools."

The battle against integration in North Carolina was led by a group called the White Patriots who included in their number three former speakers of the N. C. House. They feared, they said, that Anglo-Saxon Americans would become a "mongrel race." Naturally this breathed new life into the KKK and brought racism back to the forefront. I. Beverly Lake, a Wake

Forest law professor, became the face and voice of opposition to Hodges. He was not alone. In Washington Senator Sam Ervin helped draft a Southern Manifesto that condemned <u>Brown</u> as judicial overreach that would ultimately set back relations between blacks and whites. Both Ervin and Kerr Scott signed, followed by all but four of North Carolina's representatives in the House, one Republican and three Democrats. Three of those Democrats who didn't sign were defeated in the next election. Hodges, on the other hand, was handed a substantial victory in his reelection bid in 1956.

Hodges' next term was quieter, thus allowing him time to act as North Carolina's salesman-in-chief. Hodges was the first governor to use his office for a campaign to attract new industries to the state. He was quite successful, as industrial investment increased from $244 million in 1957-58 to $256 million in 1959-60. And these were diversified industries he attracted, like food processing, electronics and chemicals. Reacting to a feeling of increased prosperity, the General Assembly enacted a biennial budget exceeding $1 billion, an all-time high, and authorized a series of bond issues for capital construction at the universities, community colleges, state mental institutions, ports, and state training schools, and a rehabilitation center for the blind. They also passed the first minimum wage law in the South and, recognizing that the state's water needs were growing, established the Department of Water Resources to oversee water conservation.

It had been a difficult seven years, but had been rewarding as well. As Hodges had learned, at the beginning, North Carolina was far behind in wages, per capita income and college enrollment; as a new decade came, North Carolina was making progress in all those areas. After long neglecting its waters and its neediest citizens, the state's leaders turned their attention to those issues. Racial matters continued, however, to bedevil the state. The business community, which, after all was said and done, ran the state, had looked at the option of putting up massive resistance to integration and blinked: they held back. Having a fellow businessman in office who preached moderation was doubtless an influential factor. Hodges was another in the line of modern governors like Gardner, whose machine he inherited. Conservative fiscally and socially, not radical by any means, he was able to lead many North Carolinians toward a brighter future.

George L. Simpson, Jr., the first director of the Research Triangle Committee and later chancellor of the University System of Georgia, in the May 1960 issue of The University of North Carolina News Letter wrote:

> The state, which in 1945 was several times the largest industrial state in the Southeast and one of the largest in the Nation, was not making satisfactory progress in industrial growth. Ground was being lost in manufacturing wage rates. The per capita income situation had worsened. Agricultural income was beginning to level off. Out-migration was picking up. The demand for public services was growing far faster than tax receipts. It was to this crisis that the two administrations of Governor Luther Hodges have addressed themselves, to the particular need of industrial growth as the basic answer." (Lefler, 685)

The result of fifty-plus years of traditionalist policies was undeniable—underfunded schools, sparse infrastructure, poor public services, low taxes, and voter suppression had left the state struggling to compete nationally or even regionally.

CHAPTER IV
"HALF WAY HOME AND A LONG WAY TO GO"
1960 - 2010*

It was Terry Sanford – lawyer, Eagle Scout, and war hero – who launched North Carolina on its truly progressive course. He was partially defined by his opposition. As the national party moved further and further to the left, opposition within North Carolina became more and more pronounced. Many in the business community had never fully accepted the policies of FDR or Harry Truman, and now they had the issue of integration to swallow. The Democratic Party in North Carolina held on, but they were increasingly challenged by conservatives within their own ranks in addition to a growing Republican Party. Sanford would fight both those forces. He had to define himself as different from his opponents, but he also had to be constantly aware that too much change too fast would lose his public and business support. He wanted to get things done, but he was a politician, after all, and first he had to get elected. He was a risk taker who took calculated risks, thereby moving the state forward.

Sanford was a decorated World War II veteran who went on to graduate from UNC Law School. His family, who came from Laurinburg, were moderate Methodists who taught their children tolerance. Apparently they also imbued in them a significant dose of ambition. After law school, Sanford became involved in state politics. Elected to the state Senate in 1952, he was Kerr Scott's campaign manager in 1952 for the U.S. Senate; Kerr Scott wanted his campaign to be a vindication of Frank Porter Graham. That campaign, in which Smith's publicity director, Jesse Helms, had vilified the saintly "Dr. Frank" as soft on communism and not strong enough on seg-

*This was the title of the 1986 Southern Growth Policies Board report from the Commission on the Future of the South.

regation had badly rattled the more liberal of the state's Democrats, and Scott wanted revenge. However, he and Terry Sanford knew that Scott could not run on this issue of integration. So Scott bowed to reality and stated: "I have always been opposed, and I am still opposed to Negro and white children going to school together." It was a winning strategy and the populist farmer from Haw River went to the U.S. Senate.

Sanford's next goal was to run for the governorship. By 1960 the race issue, if possible, had become more emotionally charged when four African American students staged a sit-in at a Greensboro Woolworth's drug store. Soon sit-ins were spreading across the state and nation as young African Americans and some white activists demanded their civil rights. Most white North Carolinians opposed the sit-ins, with the more traditionalist seeing them as part of a Communist-inspired challenge to white supremacy. Realizing that in this atmosphere, being tagged an integrationist was a death sentence in the Democratic primary, Sanford steered to the right. He declared that he did not favor integration, but that he also didn't favor massive resistance.

His Democratic primary opponent was I. Beverly Lake, the white supremacist law professor from Wake Forrest. Among other such actions, as a way around integration, Lake had drafted legislation to remove the constitutional requirement for state-supported public schools. The campaign degenerated into a mud fight with the state's reputation on the line. Sanford wanted a "New Day;" Lake wanted a retreat to a better past that had never existed. The business community, encouraged by Luther Hodges, chose the future, putting their support behind Sanford, who went on to win the primary with 56 percent of the vote. (This kind of business support for modernization would be sorely missed in the elections of 2008 and 2010.)

Perhaps inspired by his margin of victory in the primary, Sanford then took the risky move of endorsing a young Catholic, Massachusetts Senator John F. Kennedy. Politically, it would have been wiser and safer to endorse a fellow southerner, Lyndon Johnson. But Sanford admired Kennedy, another WWII veteran, and doubled down by seconding his nomination at the national convention and openly campaigning for him. Not surprisingly, this brought out a strong wave of anti-Catholicism within the state. Still strongly fundamentalist Christians, many Tar Heels were convinced that electing Kennedy was tantamount to turning over power to the Vatican. Sanford and Kennedy crisscrossed the state together to good advantage, as Kennedy won by 52 percent and Sanford by 54.5 percent of the November vote.

It was more than a marriage of convenience; the two men genuinely liked each other. Having Sanford work closely with Kennedy for the three years he was president enhanced the image of North Carolina as a national player. There had been others who supported the national party, including Josephus Daniels, who served as Wilson's Secretary of Navy and became famous for enforcing prohibition on U.S. Naval ships years before it became law. And there was Luther Hodges, who was named U.S. Secretary of Commerce, but this was different. Sanford and Kennedy endorsed similar progressive policies and acknowledged a symbiotic relationship. Young Democrats admired the charismatic young president and his image rubbed off on Sanford, while Sanford, as a southern governor, gave respectability to Kennedy's fight for school integration in the South.

Both men were soon to be tested by African American citizens. Many young college students and ministers staged large rallies and protest marches. Sanford worried that those confrontational tactics would derail his slow and carefully modulated moves toward integration. Sanford's byword, as Hodges' had been, was "moderation." He tried to negotiate his way out of problems and was aided by the business community, which became convinced that voluntary accommodation was better than violent confrontation. Worried that violence would harm the state's hard-won image as an emerging leader in the South, the plutocracy fell in step with Sanford's accommodating policies. "In the end," wrote historian William Chafe, "Terry Sanford's positive contribution to North Carolina's race relations involved primarily the areas of atmosphere and leadership style." In other words, it was a victory of style over substance. This should not imply that it wasn't a victory, nor that a lot more was actually possible in the situation he faced, but for a state whose motto is "to be rather than to seem," it is somewhat ironic. When the nation compared the way other southern states handled their civil rights problems, North Carolina came out way ahead, thereby further advancing the state's reputation.

In some ways, it is quite surprising that North Carolina captured the attention of the nation. To be sure, Luther Hodges had been a great salesman, appearing on the cover of Life in his attempt to attract new business, and Terry Sanford encouraged federal agencies to establish facilities in the Research Triangle Park. Because of the state's expanding economy, *National Geographic* christened it in 1961 as "the Dixie Dynamo." But beneath this façade lurked some very painful and less attractive truths. North Carolina lagged in per capita income ($1,615 to US $2,254), earning only 71 percent of the national average. We had twice as many poor people as the national average and far fewer college graduates. North Carolina had made great strides since World War II but still had a long way to go. In 1960 almost 700,000 North Carolinians were functionally illiterate; 60,000 had never completed one year of school and thousands more were poorly educated. State spending for education in 1969 was $612 per pupil, lagging far behind the national average of $816 and ahead of only three southern states.

For Sanford the answer was education, not just integrated education, where the state continued to make slow but peaceful progress, but education in general. The governor realized that a large part of the problem was the stinginess of a conservative General Assembly. To advance the schools would take money and he was willing to stake his reputation on increased taxes for that purpose. He had stated that fact, at his peril, during the campaign, and followed up in his inaugural address: "If it takes more taxes to give our children this quality education, we must face that fact and provide the money," he said. To the legislators he proposed the Quality Education Program of $100 million to raise teacher salaries, improve school libraries, hire more teachers and increase school supplies.

To pay for this proposal, he proposed raising tax revenue by removing the exemption of food from sales tax. This was obviously a regressive tax, but the money had to come from somewhere. There was quiet resistance to the plan by conservative Democrats and, of course, Republicans, but it passed. Sanford, who knew that under the state constitution he couldn't stand for re-election, was intent on accomplishing all he could even if it wasn't popular. (He once told me when I became a college president, "It's great to be popular, but all you need is 51 percent.") Sanford saw that traditional public schools were not all that was needed. Luther Hodges had initiated a system of industrial training centers; Sanford built upon this foundation a strong system of community colleges.

To address poverty in a more immediate fashion, the governor established, with the help of the Ford Foundation, the North Carolina Fund, which was to create experimental projects in education, health, job training, housing and community development. It lasted for only five years, but provided not only projects in North Carolina, but also ideas for Lyndon Johnson's War on Poverty such as VISTA. To develop more qualified future leaders in the state, Sanford established the Governor's School for outstanding high school students and, so as not to leave cultural attainment out, he pushed for the creation of the N. C. School for the Arts. It was an amazing four years.

As had generally been true in the past, when not in power, the traditionalists were not far beneath the surface, nursing their grievances and plotting a return. Therefore, one should not be too impressed by the progressivism of Sanford's administration and what it portended for North Carolina. One sign of trouble was the increasing power of the Republican Party. Long marginalized, the civil rights and tax issues gave it new life. In the 1962 elections they gained seats in the Congress and in the General Assembly. In the 120-member House, the Republicans went from 15 to 21 seats and won victories at the county level, notably in large cities in the Piedmont. Even the Democrats, who dominated, were mostly not as progressive as Sanford. This became clear with the passage in 1963 of the Speaker Ban law, which was aimed squarely at the center of radicalism – Chapel Hill.

The law reflected the McCarthy-esque attitude of many in North Carolina who saw Communist conspiracies everywhere, especially in institutions of higher learning. So the best thing to do, they argued, was to keep Communists — and even those who had taken the Fifth Amendment in refusing to testify about alleged subversive activities — off the campus. Over the objections of President Friday and other university officials, legislators wrote their suspicions into law and closed the campus to all subversive outsiders.

The law didn't help North Carolina's reputation for forward thinking. Nor did the activities of the KKK. The Klan built its membership in direct response to the civil rights sit-ins and freedom rides crisscrossing the state. Never totally moribund, seeing Negroes demanding their rights drew new members to the United Klans of America. They marched and burned crosses, even on the grounds of the Executive Mansion. By the middle of the decade, a Congressional committee found that North Carolina was "by far the most active state" for the KKK. The book *Klansville, USA* stated that in the 1960s the KKK had more members in North Carolina than in all other southern states combined.

No doubt, Sanford's activism had inspired this kind of backlash and as he was leaving office, he was intent that this type of radical conservatism would not define the state. As usual, it was the Democratic primary that would decide the election. Sanford threw his support behind Richardson Preyer, a scion of the Richardson-Vicks (VapoRub) fortune with strong "liberal" tendencies. On the "conservative" side was the old race-baiter I. Beverly Lake, back again for another try. As a "moderate," the party had Dan K. Moore, a Superior Court judge from the western part of the state. Preyer won the first primary, but with less than a majority. In the second primary, required by law, Lake threw his support behind Moore, resulting in Preyer's defeat, 42 to 38 percent. The conservatives were elated, with Jesse Helms saying, "An aroused majority spoke – clearly, and finally. The people are fed up." It mattered little that Moore went on to win; Lake and Helms had put their stamp on North Carolina and they signaled that they weren't going away. Sanford was out of office, but he and his ideas would endure.

Moore was not cut in the Sanford mold. Big, slow-moving and slow talking, he was the epitome of moderation. However, North Carolina did see some significant improvements during his four years. For one thing, the 1965 General Assembly revisited the Speaker Ban law. Moore had appointed a commission to study the issue. The committee reported that such stifling of free speech was antithetical to the concept of open inquiry that is basic to a university's purpose. Consequently, UNC might lose its accreditation unless the ban was removed. The General Assembly consented to modify the legislation, although Jesse Helms and others weren't placated, remaining convinced that Chapel Hill harbored Communists, homosexuals and other social miscreants. The issue was not resolved until 1968 when a three-judge panel ruled the Ban's suppression of free speech unconstitutional.

During Moore's administration teachers' salaries were raised by 30 percent, which gives some indication of how low they were. Moore was distinctly pro-business, and encouraged and got a significant tax cut that business leaders favored.

JESSE COMES FROM BEHIND THE MICROPHONE

But it was actions outside the state that held the greatest portent and hope for the conservative forces. When John F. Kennedy was assassinated, he had left a host of unfilled promises. Foremost among them was civil rights legislation proposed partly in response to the protests that had roared across the South. It fell to Lyndon Johnson to see that promise through. Ignoring the irony of a Texas president's supporting civil rights legislation proposed by the man who had run against him for the highest office, Johnson put his big shoulders and legislative savvy behind the wheel. Watching Johnson at work once he got fully behind something was fascinating. He back-slapped, he arm-twisted, he badgered, he cajoled, he got in your face — all this, despite the fact that Johnson knew the bill would severely set back the Democratic Party in the South. Or, as he said to Bill Moyers, "We just delivered the South to the Republican Party for a long time to come" (New

Perspectives Quarterly, 1987). It was a case of "be careful what you wish for, you may get it," and Johnson was well aware of that fact.

In many ways the Civil Rights Act of 1964, which outlawed segregation in public accommodations and the 1965 Act, providing voting rights, were godsends to Jesse Helms and his traditionalist supporters in North Carolina. Here was the federal government enforcing racial mixing in places of public accommodation and otherwise upsetting the social balance just as it had during Reconstruction. To conservatives across the South, it was "government overreach," and an invitation to elect conservative Democrats — or to join the Republican Party. Jesse chose the latter course.

Helms was an interesting person, to put it mildly — in some ways kind and generous (he adopted a physically disabled child) and in other ways, rigid. He talked tough and was a bully, but could be polite, even jovial. A recent author has described him as similar to Alabama Governor George Wallace. "Like Wallace, Helms was ambitious, bold, crafty and outspoken... (he) thrived on the enemies he had made and the feathers he had ruffled." Moreover, "On a personal level, he could be a man of great charity and compassion." (Eamons, 153-154). One thing for sure, and even his opponents would agree, you never wondered whether Jesse meant what he said.

Jesse is a difficult person to characterize. To many people he was that rare politician who "told it like it was." In other words, no sugar coating, no complicated "professor talk." You always knew where Jesse stood and that was a good thing. Of course, many people didn't like where Jesse stood on issues like race, homosexuality and rabid anti-communism that led him to support dictators around the world. Just like there is a tradition in politics called "wrapping yourself in the flag" meaning invoking your patriotism at every opportunity – in the South there is/was a tradition for some politicians to "shout nigger" to avoid other issues and rile up their base. We call these tactics demagoguery and by many measures Jesse was a demagogue and a bigot. But when you explore this issue with Jesse supporters, they are quick to tell you some of the nice things Jesse did. He had great constituency services through his office and he seldom forgot a name and, of course, he adopted a disabled child. He also went to church regularly, but still in all he was a gutter-fighting politician with an ability to appeal to people's worst fears and prejudices.

But unfortunately, he was also a master organizer and planner who was able to leave an enduring legacy of arch-conservatism. More than any other politician in North Carolina he was able to lay the foundation and chart the course for those politicians who came to power in the 21st Century.

He got his start in politics during the Graham/Smith election and apparently reveled in this kind of bare-knuckle campaigning. He became the spokesman for A. J. Fletcher, who owned WRAL television in Raleigh. Fletcher, a very conservative anti-New Deal businessman, had decided he could no longer sit back and allow dominance of the news by Raleigh's News and Observer, which had changed 180 degrees since its race-baiting days at the turn of the century into one of the most modernizing newspapers in the region. He wanted a traditionalist voice, and in Jesse he got one. And according to Jesse, he got a father figure and a model.

Starting in 1960, Helms editorialized after the news every night and it was quite a show. I saw it first in 1964 when I came to North Carolina to go to Duke. It was the face of a really, really angry white man with the veins bulging in his neck and eyes threatening to pop out of his horn-rimmed glasses. That night his fight was with Chapel Hill and the Communists who were plotting there, but he had lots of other enemies: Lyndon Johnson, the NAACP, the gay lifestyle, modern women, illicit sex, progressives, liberals and Communists (whom he lumped together), New Deal welfare policies like social security and rural electrification – in short, modern life. Jesse was for states' rights, low taxes and private property and that was about it. He would have been very much at home in the 1890s.

The question was and is to what extent did he speak for North Carolina? Unfortunately, the answer is that his views were representative of some elements of the business community, the small-town farmer, the country preacher, the uneducated, the xenophobes, and the ignorant; and unfortunately there were lots of people who fit into one or more of those categories. There were also those who were simply uncomfortable with the pace of change in the mid-20th century and Jesse spoke to and for them as well. What many of these people liked about Jesse was that he simplified a complex world, got rid of the grey, didn't intellectualize, and "told it like it was." So in many ways, he epitomized the traditional side of North Carolina politics, which had been kept in check or papered over by such leaders as O. Max Gardner, Luther Hodges, Kerr Scott and Terry Sanford. Their moderation had obscured, but not eliminated, the more radical elements within the state. Those elements were still there and the worst thing Jesse did as a politician was give the negative aspect of traditionalism a veneer of respectability. Jesse had been a Democrat, but in 1972 he, like many other North Carolinians, changed his registration. He then ran for the U.S. Senate. And while he ran as a Republican, he was in fact a Tea Party/Libertarian ahead of his time. Beginning with his televised commentary, he also paved the way for talk radio entertainers and provocateurs like Glen Beck and Rush Limbaugh.

While Jesse was agitating on WRAL, the more moderate forces were holding political power in Raleigh. In the election of 1968, Bob Scott, son of Kerr Scott, won the governorship while, as a reminder of the growing power of the Republican Party, Richard Nixon carried the state, the first Republican to do so since Herbert Hoover. The General Assembly was still overwhelmingly Democratic and they passed new taxes (on cigarettes for the first time), raised teacher and college educators' salaries and passed conservation legislation. Notable in the latter category was money to protect water sources by buying land buffers. In the next session, they reorganized state government to make it more efficient and established a fiscal research division to police expenditures. Following the lead of his father, who had joined the Southern Regional Education Board, Bob Scott brought North Carolina into the Southern Growth Policies Board (SGPB). This organization, recognizing the South's economic challenges, was formed to give periodic reports of progress and share best practices. They also advocated funds for health and human services, most notably Medicaid, to help the needy pay for medical expenses. The state still lagged the nation in per capita income: in 1969, North Carolina at $2,474 ranked 41st, while the national average was $3,119.

If any election illustrated the schizophrenic nature of North Carolina politics it was that held in 1972. Richard Nixon won again and Jesse Helms went to the U.S. Senate. A Republican also won the governorship for the first time since 1896, but he, Jim Holshouser, was a very different Republican than Jesse Helms. Even stranger, a young, ambitious Democrat named Jim Hunt won the race for lieutenant governor. So, the state supported a traditionalist president, an archconservative senator, a moderate governor, and a Democrat lieutenant governor all at the same time.

THE TWO JIMS: HUNT/HOLSHOUSER

Jim Hunt seemed almost destined for a political career. He grew up in Wilson County as the son of an agricultural extension agent and a teacher. From them he learned his devotion to farming, education and the Freewill Baptist Church, later becoming a member of the Presbyterian church in Wilson. From high school on, Hunt was an overachiever, recognized by his classmates as a leader – a skinny kid with boundless energy and the ability to attract a following. He attended North Carolina State University, where he was twice elected student body president. His degree was in agricultural education with an M.S. in agricultural economics, but his heart was already in politics. He volunteered for the Sanford campaign, where he became infected with Sanford's positive modernist spirit. A law degree from Chapel Hill added to his credentials, and a stint in Nepal on a Ford Foundation grant as an agricultural advisor broadened his horizons. When he returned to North Carolina, he ran for and became president of the state's Young Democrats where he caught the eye of Governor Bob Scott. The Governor saw in him a fellow farm boy with potential.

As early as 1969, at 32 years old, Hunt had decided on a run for the lieutenant governor's post. For two years he worked the state, speaking anywhere he had a chance, meeting people, making friends across the political spectrum. Early on he decided to woo, not demonize, business interests. He leaned on his old N. C. State friends and put together a political organization of young, activist political neophytes plus the brilliant, seasoned Bert Bennett, Jr., the Winston-Salem oil distributor who had managed Sanford's campaign. By 1971 Hunt had the organization and the money in place to make a run for the lieutenant governorship. He won his primary, but watched in horror as his hero, Terry Sanford, lost in the North Carolina presidential primary to George Wallace, the arch-segregationist from Alabama. That was a straw in the wind showing the direction of North Carolina's political sentiments and a warning shot about how much liberality the state would stand. Hunt did not run as a liberal, or even as a progressive; he avoided labels and courted voters wherever he could find them. It was clear from the start that Hunt would be hard to categorize. To supporters he was a pragmatist who knew that to get anything done you first had to get elected. To detractors he was an opportunist who went with the political wind. However you saw him, it couldn't be denied that he had the gifts of a successful politician who won elections, and that was how in 1972 he became Lt. Governor Hunt, a staunch Democrat working with Republican Governor Holshouser.

Holshouser had served in the North Carolina House, rising to the position of minority leader. Balanced and personable, he chaired the state Republican Party from 1966 through 1972. Having been in the minority, he realized that compromise was essential to getting anything done. He and Hunt got along well because they were in essential agreement. Unlike today, the Lt. Governor had considerable legislative power, which Hunt exercised while presiding over the Senate, which, though packed with Democrats, was often more traditionalist than its Republican governor. Therefore, Hunt was sometimes in the awkward position of having to support Holshouser over Democratic opposition. With a combination of charm, tact and, where necessary, toughness, he struck a balance acceptable to Holshouser and most senators.

There were tough fights and Hunt didn't avoid them, thereby making it harder to see him as an opportunist. Holshouser supported a series of recommendations to protect the coastal environment, lumped together under the Coastal Area Management Act (CAMA). The powerful real estate interests along the coast recruited their (largely Democratic) elected delegations to fight the rules since they might complicate development. Hunt supported CAMA and was instrumental in getting it through the legislature. Then there was the bitter battle over the medical school at East Carolina University. Opposed by UNC President William Friday and the influential Chapel Hill lobby, it developed into one of those disputes where snobbery, practicality and political leverage collided. Hunt, an Eastern boy after all, supported the ECU bloc and helped make the medical school a reality.

When the legislature was not in session, Hunt was tirelessly crisscrossing the state giving speeches, cutting ribbons, attending meetings and churches and otherwise laying the groundwork for a run for governor. By many accounts Hunt was hyperactive. His ambition matched his energy level; lieutenant governor at 35, why not governor at 40 and then — who knew? — maybe national office. If hard work and organizational ability could get it done, there was no reason Hunt shouldn't reach for the stars. But there was that troubling bi-polar nature of North Carolina politics.

There hardly could be two different Republicans than Jesse Helms – or "Jesse," as he was usually called — and Jim Holshouser, who, as the first Republican governor elected in the 20th century, was a fair-minded centrist. When he went before the Democratic General Assembly in 1973 and "called on them to use available revenues to launch public school kindergartens, statewide, to purchase land for new state parks, to begin a system of rural healthcare clinics, to provide additional funds for community colleges and universities and to reduce the size of public school classes," one Democratic state senator said, "They've out-liberalized us." (Guillory, *Raleigh N&O*, 22 June, 9A) Not that Holshouser couldn't be partisan — he did retire a number of Democratic state employees — it was rather that he was even-handed. As one observer said, "Let's call it two-handed-politics. With their left hands Democrats and Republicans fought over partisan advantage, but while they had their political fights, with their right hands they worked to forge budgets and public policies that expanded educational opportunities and enhanced the quality of life of North Carolinians." (Guillory)

Actually, there was not a lot to differentiate Holshouser from the Democratic governors who immediately preceded him. Holshouser reached out to black voters and appealed to young people and women. He was genuinely a nice guy and people could tell that. In addition to the policies already noted, he encouraged far-sighted environmental protections. But at the same time, he didn't stray far from the traditional Republican and Democratic business-friendly policies of internal improvements to support economic growth and to attract new industries.

Indeed, Holshouser perhaps stirred more antipathy among the traditionalist Republicans led by Helms than he did among Democrats. For the traditionalists it was like Armageddon – they were the true believers and the moderates were the enemy regardless of party label. According to Carter Wrenn, Helms' political guru, "It was like there was these two separate islands. They were in the same nation, but they didn't talk." The ongoing warfare inspired Jesse to organize a formidable political machine, the National Congressional Club. This group pioneered direct mail campaigning and devised persuasive TV ads to support like-minded candidates for state offices. Meanwhile, Jesse, in Washington, even as a freshman senator, worked to spread his brand of Tea Party conservatism across the nation. He'd found a kindred spirit in California Governor Ronald Reagan and the two had plans for the future.

Our other traditionalist senator was Democrat Sam Ervin. Ervin represented the best of traditional North Carolina. He was a moderate conservative when it came to the civil liberties of mental patients, the poor, and Native Americans — as he defined those liberties under the Constitution. Yet he was a conservative when it came to opposing the civil rights of women or blacks. He fought every piece of civil rights legislation to come before the Senate between 1954, when he arrived, and 1975, when he left.

While personifying the best of North Carolina on some issues, like Senator Joseph McCarthy's censure by the Senate and presiding over the Watergate hearings against Richard Nixon, he also personified the less admirable side of North Carolina with his racial views. It was left to Jesse Helms, with his inflammatory racially charged campaign advertising, to demonstrate how much less admirable that side could be. When Jesse got to the Senate in 1973, he and Ervin made an odd pair. Beneath Ervin's courtly, gentlemanly façade lurked a courtly, gentlemanly human being; beneath Helms' courtly, gentlemanly façade lurked a much more rigid person. The contrast within North Carolina's senatorial delegation became sharper in other ways when in 1987 Sanford joined Jesse in the Senate.

In the 1976 presidential primary, Jesse Helms flexed his muscles and gave yet another demonstration of his take-no-prisoners approach. His candidate was Ronald Reagan, the ex-movie actor turned corporate pitchman. Governor Holshouser, on the other hand, supported Gerald Ford, who was filling out the disgraced Richard Nixon's term. Jesse not only helped Reagan carry the state; he also encouraged the North Carolina Republican Party to punish Holshouser by denying him an invitation to the national convention, which they did.

Back in Raleigh in 1977, the newly elected Jim Hunt was beginning his remarkable gubernatorial career. Though he would ultimately be viewed by many as the best of the North Carolina-style governors, Hunt viewed himself as a progressive. Yet he was a cautious progressive, never straying far from the old triumvirate of business, education and internal improvements. He was the consummate politician, willing to veer from the centrist path, either left or right, when the circumstances demanded. Over the years, the course was more center/left, but Hunt managed to retain the support of North Carolina's more forward-looking plutocrats in the banking and financial centers.

This didn't happen by chance. Hunt knew his history, including the central role played by the business community for good or ill. He set out in a calculating way to court those business people whom he thought vital to North Carolina's future. Early in his administration, he established the North Carolina Council on Business Management and Development. Members were selected from the biggest and most influential companies in the state; among other members were representatives of R. J. Reynolds, N.C. National Bank, Wachovia Bank, Duke Power and Carolina Power & Light. The governor met with them four times a year for socializing and exchanging ideas. Not surprisingly these men (and they were all men) nudged Hunt in a fiscally conservative direction, although it was not conservative enough for some other industrialists, particularly those in the furniture and textile business. Even so, Hunt had the support he needed to push one of his top priorities – higher wages. "We're going to put wage levels first. We need higher wages," he said. (Pearce, 112) To attract the new kind of businesses that paid those wages, Hunt established the centers for biotechnology and microelectronics in Research Triangle Park.

The big businesses and the new businesses also approved of Hunt's expending most of his energy and political capital on education. While education was not a priority for some of the old businesses, Hunt "was willing to fight an ingrained business culture that for decades hadn't seen much need for education past high school." (Pearce, 115) It was this attitude in part which had kept North Carolina so far behind in family and per capital income. In 1979 North Carolina ranked 44th in family income and 42nd in per capita income. Poorly educated workers couldn't demand high wages — they had neither the know-how nor the confidence that their efforts would do any good — hence Hunt's drive for more education as a step toward increased earning power.

The business establishment also appreciated the fact that Hunt kept a lid on civil rights issues where he could. When national attention was drawn to the much-contested conviction of the Wilmington 10, it looked as if the governor had been forced into a corner from which there was no way out. All his liberal supporters wanted a pardon, while conservatives as well as some moderates thought a pardon unjustified. There had been a riot in Wilmington, people had been killed and a court had found ten people guilty of arson and conspiracy. The Governor's political style here was perfectly illustrated by how he finessed the issue of the Wilmington 10. Instead of pardoning them, Hunt reduced their sentences, leaving it to a successor,

Beverly Perdue, to issue a gubernatorial pardon in 2012.

But as stated earlier, Hunt's primary commitment was to education; in his support of better schools, he made clear his desire to bring North Carolina into the national mainstream. With the backing of Democratic majorities in both the House and Senate, the Governor urged pouring billions of dollars into education from kindergarten through college. He recognized the importance of a good preschool experience for students, particularly low-income students. But he also realized that precocious high school students needed a place to foster their skills in science and math, so he promoted the founding of the North Carolina School of Math and Science, the first such school in the nation.

Fortunately, the issue of integration had faded nationally and in all but a few pockets of Eastern North Carolina, so, rather than having to fight over civil rights issues, Hunt was free to act on his convictions, appointing African Americans and also women to positions of responsibility.

In all these areas Hunt, as no other governor before him, was conscious of where North Carolina stood in the country. He was a farm boy, but he didn't want North Carolina regarded as a redneck, hillbilly state. He knew that North Carolina was better than that and he wanted his state to compete on a national stage for progressive honors. Specifically, he wanted to raise teacher salaries to the national average and he wanted the test scores of Tar Heel students to be among the highest in the nation. He set a high standard of personal rectitude as a teetotaling, straight-laced, perhaps a little stiff, chief executive.

He also was an adroit politician who encouraged the change in the constitution that allowed a governor to run for a second term. As soon as he was elected for his first term, he set about putting together a statewide organization intended to keep him and other Democrats in office. Sometimes using powerful members of the General Assembly and sometimes using sheriffs, the Hunt organization rivaled any ever seen in the state. Certainly there has been no such Democratic organization since he left office.

The Republicans, however, had some strong coattails in 1980, as Ronald Reagan was running again, this time against Jimmy Carter, the incumbent president, who was hurt by the Iran hostage crisis and a weak economy. Hunt's challenger was I. Beverly Lake Jr., the son of the segregationist who had run for governor in 1960. But even Reagan was not enough to defeat the popular Hunt and his organization; he won a second term with 62 percent.

Hunt was faced with two big issues – improving the highway system and increasing funding for education and teacher salaries. The business community wanted roads and the education establishment wanted increased funding. The solution was a gas tax, which would go for highway construction and repair. With the recession in the 1980s, a tax increase was a hard sell; but Hunt and his team of lobbyists were hard sellers. Willing to twist arms and to use patronage to get what he wanted, the governor set out to get a gas tax increase. As a balance, he emphasized cutting the cost of government and he did make economies where he could. When the votes in the legislature were counted, he won. But he wasn't willing to put up the same fight for teachers, thereby earning their enmity as well as tarnishing his reputation as an education advocate. But with the state in a recession, Hunt felt he either had to freeze salaries or lay off teachers. He chose to freeze their salaries despite the fact that in 1980 North Carolina was still mired in the bottom tier in education spending – only above Arkansas, Mississippi, Alabama, Kentucky and South Carolina.

Much of Hunt's attention during this second term was directed toward the future. Since he couldn't run for governor again, his eyes had turned to another prize and maybe then the biggest prize. Jesse Helms would be up for reelection in 1984; a resounding victory in a U.S.

Senate race would not only redeem North Carolina's reputation as a progressive state, but also be a step toward a presidential run.

Since Hunt could not run again for governor in 1984, the Democrats, hoping that Senator Sam Ervin's Watergate performance would rub off on his aide, nominated Rufus Edmisten. To oppose him, the Republicans united behind Jim Martin, who always liked to emphasize that he was a Davidson College chemistry professor, but who, more importantly, had been a politician for twenty years, ending up as a congressman. Described as "a business progressive who was a consensus builder," he was whip smart and tough. Rufus couldn't do a convincing imitation of Senator Sam and then there was again the influence of Reagan. This time his coattails worked and Jim Martin became North Carolina's second Republican governor in the 20th century.

Martin first displayed his toughness by turning out hundreds of Democratic office holders; then he showed his political acumen by backing a $1 billion bond issue for school and road construction. He steered clear of the integration issue, although he personally favored a moderate forward movement. Being business-friendly, he didn't challenge the anti-union right-to-work law, and he said little about higher wages. He was a practical, not dramatic governor who didn't stray far from the center of the road; he clearly was not a radical ideologue, instead he was a thoughtful moderate. Under his leadership the state moved gradually forward.

HUNT/HELMS

Martin's win may also have been helped by the real political contest of 1984 – Hunt versus incumbent Helms for the U.S. Senate. At first the race looked easy: Hunt was ahead in the polls and Jesse seemed vulnerable. But Jesse had the Congressional Club, with its money and its talent for direct mail and TV advertising, and those Democrats who liked Jesse – Jessecrats, they were called. The first change in the polls came when Jesse began to use the Senate floor to attack the Martin Luther King, Jr. holiday initiative. Jesse reverted to his WRAL style, attacking King as anti-American and in league with the Socialists and the Communists. As Helms well knew, the race card always played well with a segment of North Carolinians. It was the Smith/Graham race of 1950 all over again with the Helms organization willing to use smears, innuendo and outright lies. Hunt supported the King holiday against the advice of his campaign manager and, thereby, lost some of his supporters.

The Helms campaign next brought up the volatile issue of homosexuality. Hunt had homosexual friends, and might even be homosexual himself, they implied. An article in a free weekly newspaper, from which the Helms organization never completely distanced itself, was headed "Jim Hunt is Sissy, Prissy, Girlish and Effeminate." There was no substance to the story, but that was not nearly as important as winning.

Not that Hunt wasn't willing to take the gloves off — his attacks centered on Jesse's support for brutal dictators in Latin America and elsewhere. To these charges there was substance. Jesse had a lot of unsavory friends in El Salvador, Chile, Nicaragua, and Argentina who, in Hunt's view, resorted to any means as long as they were anti-Communist. Helms responded, naturally, by claiming Hunt was not anti-Communist enough and was even soft on Socialists. And nobody could match Jesse on anti-communism; even Richard Nixon was not tough enough. Ronald Reagan came close to Jesse's ideal and he visited North Carolina to campaign for his friend. Hunt's campaign was urged to use the abortion issue against Helms, who naturally was an outspoken opponent of <u>Roe v. Wade</u>, but Hunt demurred, even though outlawing abortion was not popular in North Carolina. Jesse didn't demur from crisscrossing the state talking about Hunt's support from homosexuals, labor unions and black-bloc voters.

In the end Jesse won 52 to 48 percent, thus, again illustrating the tendency of North Carolinians to support modernizers while never completely abandoning traditional values. It was a humiliating defeat for Jim Hunt, who took it very hard. For the state it was the Graham/Smith defeat all over again. In this bellwether race, Helms took the blue collar, middle income, and evangelicals; Hunt took the college educated, minority, and moderate voters. The Republican Party took note; this election could have national implications. An archconservative defeating a popular progressive on his own North Carolina turf was a step forward for the Republicans' plan to take the South. And it destroyed any hopes that Hunt may have had for running for president.

In 1986 the Southern Growth Policies Board, which was housed in the Research Triangle Park, approved a progressive agenda for the region. With the full support of Governor Martin, their agenda included providing "a nationally competitive education for all southern students..." preparing a "flexible, globally competitive workforce..." increasing "the economic development role of higher education" and increasing the South's "capacity to generate and use technology..." North Carolina was committed to moving into the 21st century.

In 1988 Martin won another term as governor and continued along his moderate ways: tax cuts for businesses, reorganizing state government to make it more efficient, and money for schools. And then in Martin's last year in office, an increase would come in the gas tax in order to build more roads. But he also sensed that the Democratic control of the House could be challenged. Liston Ramsey from rural Madison County in the mountains had been speaker for eight years, wielding considerable power, but the Republicans had been slowly eating away at the majority's numbers. In 1989 Martin and the Republicans staged a successful coup by recruiting 19 Democrats who had bridled under Ramsey's rule, and replaced him with the less dictatorial Joe Mavretic. It was the beginning of a Republican campaign to win control of the House.

IT'S HUNT AGAIN

In 1992, restless after being out of office for eight years, Jim Hunt, the two-time governor, decided to give it another go. He had an agenda. "I wanted to change the country," he said, "But I figured the best way to do that was to build a state that would be America's model. It was burning in me to change North Carolina, to make North Carolina a model state in America." His opponent would be Jim Gardner, who had first run for governor in 1968. Gardner also wanted to change North Carolina – to take it back to its more conservative past. His constituency was the Helms following of old Democrats as well as some of the conservative Republican business base. The battle lines again were drawn in their familiar locations — the traditionalist East versus the more modernizing central part of the state

Hunt drafted an agenda for action emphasizing the old themes of education, economic development and crime control; the latter intended to appeal to the more conservative member of his base. Although Gardner was a businessman, in that he had started a line of hamburger restaurants, the more enlightened members of the business community knew Jim Hunt and knew that he had a record of supporting business growth. Gardner got some of Jesse's voters, but with the teachers and the college-educated voters behind him, Hunt went on to a resounding victory.

But as a warning that forces of conservatism were still there, the traditionalists won their own victory in 1992. Lauch Faircloth, a former Democratic secretary of commerce in Hunt's first administration, ran as a Republican for the Senate against an aging and ailing Terry Sanford. Faircloth won and announced that now Jesse Helms would be "the liberal senator from North Carolina." (Pearce, 229)

In this, his third term as governor, Hunt drove particularly hard on his early childhood education program. He was convinced that an early start was essential and that many children, especially low-income children, weren't getting the help they needed, so he titled his program "Smart Start." The program became a national model. The governor had also vowed to get tough on crime and, over the opposition of some of his more modernist supporters, he set about doing so. Part of the problem was that getting tough on crime meant getting tough on inmates and law breakers who were disproportionately black, but a vow was a vow and, in fact, while out of office Hunt had become more traditionalist on some issues, including crime control. Democrats in the House dragged their feet, but ultimately Hunt got his way.

His more traditionalist tilt came about in part because of his finely attuned political sense for sniffing the wind. The Republican Party was on a rampage against President Bill Clinton, who had been elected the same year Jim Hunt had. In the Republican landslide of 1994 they swept the board, taking both houses of Congress. In North Carolina they captured the State House for the first time in the 20th century, but these weren't the old Reconstruction Republicans; these were fiscally conservative, country club, business friendly Republicans. Though not the Tea Party Republicans elected in 2010, they would be, or had the potential to be, a real thorn in Hunt's side.

But they may have misjudged just how flexible and nimble the governor could be. Sensing that one of the House's priorities would be tax cuts, Hunt set about out-bidding them. His attitude was, "You want a tax cut, I'll give you a bigger tax cut," what he proposed was a really big tax cut. Thinking that the state was prosperous enough to afford it, he put forward half a billion dollars in tax cuts. But he balanced repeal of the intangible tax on stocks and bonds, a move that appealed to the wealthy, with a repeal of the state sales tax on food, while increasing income-tax exemptions, which appealed to the middle class. The Republicans were outflanked and had to go along whether they supported the whole package or not – after all, it was a tax cut, which they ideologically favored. Hunt would later admit that he had gone too far, but at the time it helped solidify his business support. (Pearce, 240)

That support had grown more and more important in Hunt's mind. In his years out of office, he had worked closely with businessmen in his law practice. He had come to know them better and found that he liked many of them. Moreover, they were valuable political allies. "When business people spoke, average citizens listened to them. People just trusted them and so did most legislators." (Pearce, 242) It was his belief that the old-fashioned plutocrats of the textile and furniture industries had been replaced by a more modernizing type; "They were conservative, but they cared about issues like education and economic change." (Pearce, 243) So the Democratic Party, as it had been for the past century, was content to serve the interests of the business community, and the support of that community was essential to advancing a progressive agenda. It was a symbiotic relationship. There is no doubt they helped gain Republican support in the House for Hunt's agenda.

One issue that Hunt's General Assembly agreed upon was the establishment of the Progress Board. This was a non-partisan board established in 1995 by the General Assembly to track developments in areas that affected public life. The legislators and the Governor wanted to set goals in eight areas and measure progress relative to that made in the region and the country.

When 1996 came around Hunt was again on the ticket. This time he ran against a traditionalist member of the N.C. House, Robin Hayes, who owned a hosiery mill. Hayes was very much a member of the old textile plutocracy; his mother was the daughter of the textile magnate Charles Cannon. In the primary, Hayes had used the abortion issue prominently, citing his Republican opponent, Richard Vinroot's, support of Planned Parenthood as an indication of his lack of ideological purity. This, among other things, made the Hunt people believe that Hayes' traditionalism and focus on social issues would not sit well with the majority of North Carolina's voters. They were right: Hunt was swept into office for an unprecedented fourth term. Some would suggest that he ran a more traditionalist campaign than he needed to by wooing the National Rifle Association, (NRA) and fundamentalist ministers, but he wanted to win big.

The main thing he emphasized was teacher salaries. With his work at the national level on education, Hunt had become convinced that good teachers were vital to student success. So, if you wanted to improve students' scores on tests and to turn out a competitive product, you needed to attract and retain good teachers. Salaries weren't everything, but when you were losing half your teachers after five years, salaries might help keep some of them. Furthermore, teachers should be rewarded for getting advanced degrees and attaining certification. To reach his goal, Hunt mobilized his friends in the business community and brought them to Raleigh to meet with legislators. When leaders of the 15 largest employers in North Carolina speak, legislators listen. It can't be known whether they were the deciding factor, but by the time Hunt left office, North Carolina teacher pay almost reached the national average. It was a success that raised North Carolina's profile and doubtless raised its reputation as a good place to send your kids to school and maybe establish your business. Between 1990 and 2000, North

Carolina was the fastest growing state in the southeast, except for Georgia, and was the fifth fastest growing in the nation.

Jim Hunt was, as the century ended, very much the public face of North Carolina. In power for a total of 16 years, he pushed the state forward, never losing sight of the need for education, new industry and equal opportunities for blacks and for women. Inspired by him, many others took up the task of building North Carolina into a national example of how a southern state could change, never losing its southern-ness, but instead joining and sometimes leading national trends. Hunt's eye was always on the future and he thought North Carolina could be a big part of that future. He changed with the times, as he had to if he expected to lead. As Ferrell Guillory put it, "Jim Hunt's achievement was to figure out how to survive in the changing economy and the changing political landscape of the South and still remain a Democrat... He picked his spots. He broadened his base. Yet he remained a Democrat." By doing so, he provided a good model for another southerner, Bill Clinton, who led the nation through similar changing times.

In this changing environment, it is perhaps surprising the Democrats continued to do as well as they did. Once back in power in the General Assembly in 1999, they held on for 12 years. The most powerful man in the Senate was President Pro Tem Marc Basnight from the Outer Banks. Although sometimes derided because of his accent and lack of formal education, Basnight was an adroit politician who was able to command the loyalty of the shifting coalitions within his party. Basnight always looked out for the sometimes narrow interests of his region, like the commercial fishermen, but he had wider interests as well. He was a protector to the university system, which was often attacked by members of the North Carolina House. He was a strong advocate of environmental interests on matters such as clean water. And while he well understood and often worked closely with business interests, he was always a populist. Basnight was ably assisted in the Senate by majority leader Tony Rand. The House was not as tightly controlled; in 2003-2004 the numbers of seats held by the two parties were so close that there were co-speakers. Then the Democrats gained total control again and held it until 2010, when huge change would come.

It may be an overstatement, but Democratic policies were more clearly reflected in the General Assembly during the first ten years of the 21st century than in the Governor's Mansion. Mike Easley, who was elected in 2000, and again in 2004, was a very unusual politician who had the advantage of running against relatively weak opponents. Easley had no machine and in fact ran without the support of the Democratic power structure. His reputation was that of a crime-fighting attorney general who, while serving as district attorney, ran considerable personal risks putting criminals behind bars. Maybe it was the contrast between the Elliot Ness background and the mild-mannered Clark Kent persona that won the election, because Easley was anything but a dynamic campaigner. However, it has been observed that he knew how to "connect with ordinary voters, including white males, who often shunned Democratic candidates. He had a plain, unassuming style and a fondness for stock car racing." (Eamons, 265)

He carried the same manner into the governorship. He was in some ways an outsider, who leaned heavily on his wife for the warm, fuzzy aspects of the office. He slept late, gave short speeches and didn't really like crowds, even partisan crowds. His primary achievements were in the area of education, where his "More at Four" program for at-risk pre-kindergarten children won national recognition. He also raised teacher salaries and championed an innovative program for on-line learning. Easley also deserves credit for bringing attention to the economic and social disparity that existed between rural North Carolina and the rest of the state. In his acceptance speech, he said, "We cannot have two North Carolinas. Our economy is on a roll in this state but it must roll over every citizen in every town." But we did and we still do have two North Carolinas, roughly divided between those on the east side of I-95 and those on the west, with some pockets of poverty in the Piedmont and the mountains. However, his administrations were burdened with the lack of revenue to address the inequality brought about in part by the Hunt tax cuts.

Given the fact that Easley was willing to highlight the "two North Carolinas," his reaction to the 2006 Progress Board Report, assessing quality of life in the state, was a little hard to understand. As the report was being prepared, one of his political advisors attended many of the meetings, generally looking for ways to soften the critical conclusions. He was particularly unhappy with the grading system that was used as a measure of success or need for progress as compared to other states. In response, the grading system was modified several times. It wasn't enough; Easley decided the reports from this board were making his administration look bad. For example, the score given in the area of "healthy children and families" was C-; infrastructure got a D+. (A report summary is in the Appendix. Full disclosure: I was interim executive director of this board.)

While the report could be read as not reflecting well on Governor Easley, board members tried to convince him that he was not responsible for the problems, nor was he expected to fix them all. The report was intended to track progress in eight important areas. By showing lack of progress, the intent was to direct attention and funding to these areas. What the report called for was emphasis on all those areas where the state was not doing well. And to be sure, there were those areas. It was to no avail; in the end he appointed a trusted advisor as chairman and then allowed the organization to be defunded. But dealing with the Progress Board was easy compared to some of his other problems.

The state suffered from a downturn in the economy in Easley's second term, and with his support, the General Assembly raised taxes several times to cover budget shortfalls – never a popular move. But even more burdensome were the mistakes Easley and his wife made. North Carolina had always had a reputation for good government, at least in terms of senior administrative officials mostly staying out of scandals. Easley broke new ground on that front by becoming the first North Carolina governor to take an Alford Plea, implying that he could be convicted of committing a felony. Apparently the governor made the not-uncommon mistake of lack of attention to filing campaign finance reports, which became an embarrassment compounded by his soliciting a high-salaried job for his wife. The scandal so dominated the last years of his administration that he left office in disgrace.

A HARD TURN TO THE RIGHT

With Easley's troubles, the Republicans saw a real opportunity to seize control of the state. The mayor of Charlotte, Pat McCrory, seemed the perfect candidate to take over the governor's office. A 28-year executive with Duke Power, he had the business credentials that had proved helpful in the past. He had served 14 years as the moderate mayor of the state's largest city, and the fact that Charlotte was also the banking capital shouldn't hurt when it came to raising money. Running on the Democratic ticket was Lt. Governor Beverly Perdue. The consummate insider, Perdue had worked her way up through the N. C. House and then in the Senate as an able lieutenant to Marc Basnight. She had proved herself a tough-minded politician, willing to do what it took to move up in the ranks of the "old-boy network" (Eamons, 306). Perdue would also be running as the first female gubernatorial candidate, a considerable burden in North Carolina. Finally, and this gave the Republicans real hope, the Democratic nominee for president was the mixed-race senator from Illinois, Barack Obama. But the most helpful thing was the start of the Great Recession. By clever campaign strategy the Republicans sought to show that the economic fate of the country was in the hands of the Democrats in Raleigh.

Traditionalist forces within the state rallied behind McCrory and for Obama's opponent, John McCain. Playing an increasing role on the conservative side was Art Pope and his John Locke Foundation. Pope is the wealthy one-man force carrying on Jesse Helms' legacy. While he appears to be a mild-mannered, rumpled-suit, small-town businessman, he is a tough fisted opponent.

Most North Carolinians had never heard of Art Pope, despite the fact that he has been a conservative force in the state and the country since the mid-1980s. When the Koch brothers founded Citizens for a Sound Economy in 1984 they put Pope on the board, a position he currently holds with their Americans for Prosperity group. Over the last ten years Pope and his foundation have given $35 million to six "ostensibly nonpartisan" policy organizations. Taking advantage of changes in tax and campaign finance laws, a recent article contends that, "he has created a singular influence machine that…blurs the lines between tax-deductible philanthropy and corporate-funded partisan advocacy." There are those who see Pope as the kingmaker in North Carolina. As a Democratic consultant said, "In a very real sense, Democrats running for office are always running against Art Pope. The Republican agenda in North Carolina is really Art Pope's agenda. He sets it, he funds it, and he directs the efforts to achieve it." (Jane Mayer, "State for Sale: A Conservative Multimillionaire has taken control of North Carolina…" (*New Yorker Magazine*, October 10, 2011)

The Foundation is a think tank Pope founded in 1990, which took on some of the trappings of Helms' old Congressional Club. According to its mission statement, it "employs research, journalism, and outreach programs to transform government through competition, innovation, personal freedom and personal responsibility." The John Locke Foundation "seeks a better balance between the public sector and private institutions of family, faith, community and enterprise." In other words, less government, less welfare, and more private enterprise all wrapped up in religion and small town values. With the exception of religion and small-town values, it sounds very much like what North Carolina's traditionalists had been bent on for at least fifty, maybe 100 years. If there was anything they would welcome it was a race against a female lieutenant governor and an African American U.S. senator.

It seemed too good to be true and it was. Defying all logic and all expectations, Obama narrowly carried the state and almost as significantly, Beverly Perdue became North Carolina's first female chief executive. Swept into senatorial office was Kay Hagan, who handily defeated Elizabeth Dole. The North Carolina General Assembly remained firmly in Democratic hands.

Almost immediately it became clear that Beverly Perdue would suffer as a result of lingering suspicions about Easley and his staff. Then there was her own scandal; there were allegations of improper campaign spending for which Perdue's campaign was ultimately fined $30,000. Within six months she was seen as one of the most unpopular governors in the nation. The unemployment situation that lingered through her term in office also didn't help. The idea began to circulate that she wouldn't have won in the first place had it not been for Barack Obama's surprise in carrying the state. And while it has been said that she was "surpassed by none in determination," (Eamons, 307) she found it increasingly difficult to raise money. The Republicans, on the other hand, began to plan for the next election when there would be no national coattails. Finally, in January 2012, she announced that she would not seek reelection.

With the incumbent not seeking reelection it offered an even better opportunity for Art Pope, North Carolina's version of the nationally famed wealthy supporters of conservative causes, the Koch brothers. Pope controls the $150 million Pope Family Foundation built with funds from Variety Wholesalers, a discount store conglomerate. Though he had founded the John Locke Foundation, it was not until 2006, when he gained control over the Pope Family Foundation, that he became a real kingmaker. Pope's power has grown in direct contrast to the diminution of the Democratic Party organization. In the view of Katrina vanden Heuvel, a prominent liberal journalist, "Pope and his cash are responsible for North Carolina's recent meteoric rise as the poster child for regressive, conservative politics." She goes on, "with money to burn, Pope and his cronies are on their way to turning state after state into regressive backwaters" while using their money to drown out the opposition. (Katrina vanden Heuval, Washington Post, June 11, 2013).

When one talks about the John Locke Foundation, it is easy to dismiss it as just another think tank, but it is part of an organizational octopus. There is the Civitas Institute, which does polling, sponsors events, publishes research, provides material to media, encourages grassroots advocacy and trains interns. Their mission is to "facilitate the implementation of conservative policy solutions to improve the lives of North Carolinians." They focus on a wide range of issues, including budget and taxes, corruption and ethics, economy, education, elections and voting, environment, healthcare, justice and public safety, legislative activity and family issues. Then there is the foundation's *Carolina Journal*, which prints a monthly newsletter, has a weekly radio show, and provides clips to TV stations on conservative subjects. As if this were not enough, there is a separate Pope Center for Higher Education Policy which issues critical studies of the university system.

Starting in 2006, Pope determined to force moderate Republicans out of the General Assembly. According to an article by Jane Mayer in *The New Yorker*, "He sent out a clear message to the Republican moderates: if they didn't heed him, he would not hesitate to go after them." He created a "climate of fear." Chris Kromm, the executive director of the Institute for Southern Studies said, "He has a whole network that can reward or punish Republicans... That's the strength of the Pope network. It enforces ideological conformity, and gets people in line... He just keeps pushing this far-down-the-spectrum view relentlessly, until it's viewed as the common consensus."

CHAPTER V
"LET'S GO BACKWARD" 2010 – 2014
THE REDEEMERS COME AGAIN

The Citizens United decision, handed down in January 2010 by the U.S. Supreme Court, was a Godsend to Art Pope. In a reversal of precedent, a bitterly divided Supreme Court ruled that the government could not ban campaign spending by corporations or unions. Pope quickly set up groups to which he could funnel money and from whom he could solicit contributions. There were Real Jobs North Carolina and the North Carolina branch of Americans for Prosperity, on which he held a board seat. Then he had Civitas Action, which could and did back candidates and produce attack ads. Recognizing Pope as a very valuable ally, the national Republican Party sent one of its senior operatives, Ed Gillespie, to visit in the spring of 2010. Gillespie spent the day recruiting Pope to be part of REDMAP, a plan for taking over the state legislature. It didn't take much convincing.

Who ever heard of the Republican State Leadership Committee (RSLC)? It is little-known and yet has been crucial in moving the state rightward. Founded in 2002, the RSLC is the largest caucus of Republican state leaders in the country and the only national organization whose mission is to elect "down ballot, state-level Republican office holders." (RSLC.com) They focus on the office of lieutenant governor, attorney general, secretary of state and state legislators. Of immense help to the RSLC in North Carolina was the Citizens United decision, which made it possible for corporate interests and political action committees (PACS) to reach into the state elections, pick and then fund particular candidates. In 2010 the RSLC raised $28 million as part of their state-directed war chest. Millions of those dollars flowed into North Carolina.

By spring 2010 the RSLC had spun off another project, the RED-STATE effort. Led by Gillespie, the REDSTATE project targeted states where they thought Republicans could take over the Senate. It wasn't just control of the legislatures they sought – they wanted control over redistricting. Looking at how close the 2008 election had been, they determined that North Carolina was a state where the Senate was within reach. Naturally Art Pope and his associates worked closely with REDSTATE, targeting 22 races and pouring $2.2 million into them. In addition, outside groups like the RSLC and other PACS working with Pope put in 75 percent of the independent spending in the targeted races. In total they poured $10 million into North Carolina. Nationally, the RSLC and its money helped flip North Carolina and 18 other states. In North Carolina, REDSTATE candidates won in 18 out of the 22 targeted races, seizing control of the state Senate.

On Election Day, November 2, 2010, the Republicans swept the board, taking over the House and the Senate. It was widely reported that this was the first time that the Republicans controlled the General Assembly since they were removed from power in 1898. That is nonsense; it was all a matter of semantics since the traditionalists, who were then the Democrats, had held power from 1870 – 1894 and then again from 1898 through the first fifty years of the 20th century; the difference was only as deep as party labels. In the 19th century, until about 1950, the traditionalists were the Democrats – after 1950, the traditionalists were the Republicans.

What to call these new people? They are not the "traditionalists" who had once populated the Democratic and Republican parties. These people are more ideological and in some ways more clever than their predecessors. They also are more willing to take their lead from out-of-state operatives. Nationally, analysts are struggling to find a way to label. Some of these new office holders or office seekers are clearly appealing to the Tea Party (Ted Cruz, Josh Hensarling, Mike Brat), while many of them only solicit support from the Tea Party when convenient; like Eric Cantor who rode the tiger hoping it would eat him last, but also have traditionalist characteristics. Some have used the term "establishment" when trying to differentiate between

Tea Party candidates and those a little more to the left, but that is becoming increasingly imprecise. All Republican candidates have to give lip service to the Tea Party or risk a violent backlash.

Tom Tillis is a perfect example. He won the Republican primary in May so he will face Kay Hagan in November. As the *New York Times* put it, he was the "establishment" candidate, but only because establishment has been redefined to include "adamant adherence of a right-wing ideology." They go on to say, "Mr. Tillis cut federal employment benefits, and refused to pay back what the state owed Washington, leaving North Carolina to become the only state at the time to lose long-term benefits. He cut back on education spending, prompting many talented teachers to leave the state, and repealed the Racial Justice Act, which gave death-row inmates a shot at proving they were victims of discrimination. He allowed new restrictions on abortion, blocked the expansion of Medicaid and rewrote the tax code for the benefit of the rich. He and his colleagues imposed also one of the most restrictive voter ID requirements in the nation, intended to keep Democratic voters, including minorities and the poor, away from the polls." (*New York Times*, May 7, 2014).

I choose to call them "redeemers" like those white supremacists who took over the state in 1898 called themselves. As I seek to make clear, they aren't your Republican traditionalists, they are more backward yearning. They have their briefcases full of legislation fashioned for them by ALEC and brimming with bad ideas. Things like Reaganomics, trickle-down economics, nativism and creationism. And, they are zealous. One is reminded of the Yeats poem "The Second Coming," a line of which goes – "The best lack all conviction while the worst are filled with passionate intensity." But the question hangs in the wind, where are those best, the traditional Republicans who contributed so much to the state?

In any case, the Redeemers had won and as the new House majority leader said, "We are going to govern in a different way. We're going to govern in a frugal way, a responsible way." (*N&O* 3 Nov. 2010)

Whether it was responsible or not is up for debate but no one questions that it was different. Even though the Republicans had campaigned on a jobs agenda, the most obvious movement in that regard was attacking state employees, including teachers who were referred to snidely as "government teachers." They also claimed that they were making the state more "business friendly" by gutting environmental regulations. As the League for Conservation Voters saw it, "The current General Assembly leadership has pursued an unprecedented and aggressive anti-regulatory agenda. This agenda has threatened to undo many of North Carolina's major environmental achievements of the past 40 years." The new budget cut funding for the Department of Environmental and Natural Resources appointed a "business-friendly" director, decreased the buffers around water sources, and undermined the health-based clean air legislation.

Dramatic as these changes were, it was the denial of sea-level rise that made national news. The Coastal Resources Commission, which operated under CAMA, had recommended that coastal counties consider sea-level rise in their long-range plans. Science deniers in the General Assembly, taking their lead from coastal developers, put an end to that idea, prohibiting such planning until there was *proof* that the seas were rising. They also passed legislation prohibiting the state from adopting any regulations that were more restrictive than federal legislation. This was done to undo North Carolina's clean air laws. And, in general, according to the N. C. Free Enterprise Foundation, they acted to "curb the enactment of burdensome regulations on the state's citizens and businesses." Governor Beverly Perdue did what she could to put the brakes on, issuing 15 vetoes, but the Redeemers momentum was too great.

Aside from attacking teachers and dramatically cutting the appropriation for the University of North Carolina, they also went after the SREB. Among other things, that organization had established a "common market" between the 16 member states that allowed students to take courses at in-state rates if their home university did not offer a similar course of study. This was extremely helpful to many students and their parents, but as a result of the

General Assembly's 2011 Appropriation Act, North Carolina voted to no longer participate. Nothing, it seems was too small to escape their economic broom.

The Redeemers majority expended a lot of effort on social issues like abortion and gay marriage. In the latter case, the General Assembly proposed a North Carolina constitutional amendment banning gay marriage and certain types of civil unions, which voters approved in the 2012 landslide. A law mandating the use of vaginal probes prior to abortion was passed then modified while the proposal that the state establish our own currency was dropped

Gillespie and REDMAP had chosen wisely and the newly elected General Assembly went about redistricting the state. The Democrats had played the same game when they were in power, but the Redeemers did it better. Soon after the 2010 election, they put together a team of lawyers who, using mapping software, set about designing voting districts to add to the newly elected Republican majority and keep it in power for the next ten years – and survive legal challenges. A recent article in the *Washington Post* revealed that North Carolina has the most gerrymandered district in the country (the 12th District) as well as two other North Carolina districts in the top ten. They used the district lines as virtual fortresses behind which to protect Republican legislators. Once inside these districts, the elected officials need fear no liberal or even moderate challenger. Not only that, they don't need to fear the majority of the state voters. That fact was borne out in the 2012 election, when Democrats cast 50.6 percent of the votes to 48.7 percent by the Republicans in the congressional races, yet won only four out of 13 seats in the U.S. House. REDMAP had paid off.

From the Redeemers perspective, the General Assembly more than met expectations. The Redeemers had lots of targets, particularly those like the Clean Water Trust Fund, which had been the brainchild of Senator Marc Basnight. And, in one sense their outpouring of legislation was rather remarkable; how did these legislators, many of them neophytes, turn out so much legislation so fast? One explanation was part of Jesse Helms' legacy

– the American Legislative Exchange Council (ALEC). The arrangement is a bit incestuous. Jesse Helms had been one of the early members of ALEC; Art Pope had become a member of the board and had been waiting in the wings when the Republicans came into control. Like him or hate him, you have to admire Helms' long-range thinking. From the 1950s election, when he helped sully Frank Porter Graham's reputation; to his Tea Party-style commentary on WRAL; to the Senate, where he cemented his relationship with Ronald Reagan; to the bare-knuckled campaigns against Terry Sanford and Jim Hunt; to racist speeches on the Senate floor; Jesse was like the anchor holding back North Carolina's progressive efforts. In the view of one author, he was one of those rare individuals who was a "mass leader" changing history. (Eamons, 282) He was always there preaching segregation, fear, and anti-Communism, all wrapped in a mantle of free enterprise, church, and small government. Art Pope was the sorcerer's apprentice, a Jesse-ite who shared his views but without seeking the limelight. But he had ALEC and his foundations to do the politics and the arm-twisting.

Most people have never heard of ALEC, but they should have. It claims to be non-partisan yet it states up front that it is "for conservative state lawmakers who share a common belief in limited government, free markets, federalism, and individual liberty." The members believe "that government closest to the people was fundamentally more effective, more just and a better guarantor of freedom than the distant, bloated federal government in Washington, D.C." Hardly a nonpartisan comment. Jesse Helms was present at their first meeting in 1973 and later served on their board. When Reagan was elected, he took great interest in ALEC and in 1981 set up the Coordinating Task Force on Federalism, which worked closely with ALEC members. Out of that association grew the Cabinet Task Forces. The concept was to draft model legislation that could be furnished to state legislators detailing methods for "decentralizing government from the federal to the state level." In other words, it was a clearinghouse for conservative legislation. By their calculation, they furnish 1,000 such model bills a year that are introduced in the state legislatures, where over 20 percent of them have become law. ALEC claims that it has "amassed an unmatched record of achieving ground-breaking changes in public policy." They certainly could cite North Carolina as an example.

What those behind ALEC and REDSTATE and REDMAP clearly realized was that by picking off enough of those targets of opportunity they ultimately could control the Congress.

THE 2012 ELECTION

The election of 2012 turned into another solid victory for the new Redeemers. McCrory, who had been narrowly defeated by Bev Perdue in 2008, this time ran against Lt. Governor Walter Dalton. Dalton was a thoroughly decent person who unfortunately lacked flair; moreover, his campaign got a late start because Perdue did not decide not to run until January. His record, particularly in regard to education, was solid, but he never captured the public imagination. He was also hurt by having to spend money in a primary when money was hard for Democrats to come by. They held neither chamber of the General Assembly and Governor Perdue became a lame duck once she announced that she would not seek reelection. People like to give to incumbents in part because of patronage and in part because incumbents are more likely to win; but, being in the minority, the Democrats had no patronage to offer and with redistricting, victory would be very difficult.

For the Redeemers, it was helpful to have Obama on the top of the ticket. Both parties sensed that North Carolina was a bellwether state; the Democrats held their national convention in Charlotte, while the Koch brothers and their allies poured money into Republican races. The Tea Party revved up efforts, paying particular attention to "Obamacare," which they portrayed as a government takeover of healthcare — clearly an illustration of socialism run rampant despite the fact that it was based on a Republican idea. Dr. Greg Brannon, an OB-GYN in Cary, published newsletters and appeared on conservative radio shows testifying how bad "Obamacare" was going to be: the idea being that he was a doctor and he ought to know.

The lack of money, disorganization, weak candidates and, most of all, redistricting, led to another Republican landslide. To be sure, the anemic economy didn't help, as the Republicans again campaigned on the premise that the economic problems were rooted in Raleigh. Romney brought North Carolina back into the Red State ranks at the presidential level; McCrory beat Dalton 54 percent to 43.2 percent. On the congressional side, Redeemers won nine out of the 13 districts despite the fact that more Democratic votes were cast by the state's voters, 50.6 percent supported Democrats while only 48.7 percent supported Republicans. In the General Assembly the Redeemers increased their hold in both the House and the Senate, and both bodies became much more Tea Party-like. Though it was hard to believe, this General Assembly made the 2010-2011 General Assembly appear moderate.

McCrory had campaigned on a platform that declared North Carolina was broken and he was going to fix it. As the Progress Board Report had suggested, North Carolina did have problems that needed fixing, but this wasn't where McCrory focused his efforts. One of his first acts was to appoint Art Pope as budget director ("In North Carolina, Conservative donor, Art Pope, sits at the heart of government helped transform." *Washington Post*, July 19, 2014). This was an ominous sign that the budget was going to get a John Locke Foundation makeover.

McCrory and his allies attacked state government, one of the few areas where the Progress Board found North Carolina doing well – in government efficiency, the state got a C+, with a rank of 20th nationally; in state government performance a B with a rank of 16th; state government stewardship a B+ with a rank of 11th. The Redeemers leadership said more needed to be done to attract businesses, though in the economic climate category, North Carolina already ranked 5th nationally with a grade of A+, and in manufacturing vitality ranked 8th with a grade of A. Meanwhile, they undermined environmental rules, an area in which the state had earned a grade of F, and neglected infrastructure spending, where we earned a D+. And, paradoxically, they made voter participation more difficult though we had already had the low grade of a C- and a rank of 35th. (See Progress Board

Report Summary and reference in Appendix)

When I say a leap backward, look at the way in which they replayed themes drawn from the late 19th century. Voter suppression was high on their list. Disingenuously claiming they were trying to eliminate voter fraud, they crafted a voter identification plan that has been called among the most regressive in the country. With the help of ALEC they crafted a law clearly aimed at reducing voting by blacks and by young voters. Not content with that, they reduced the time for early voting and did away with voter education for the young.

Mickey Michaux, the longest serving member of the North Carolina House and a veteran of civil rights demonstrations, said we have, "voted and died for and struggled for our right to vote. You can take these 57 pages of abomination (the voter suppression law) and confine them to the streets of Hell for all eternity."

Taxes had always been an issue and they had assured their voters that they would lower them – and lower them they did. The prime beneficiaries were corporations and the wealthy. The Republicans enacted a flat tax, which eliminated a lot of exemptions like the deduction for healthcare previously enjoyed by the elderly. All in all the cuts left North Carolina with a budget incredibly designed to be in deficit. Recognizing that without funds, the government couldn't do much, they were following the Grover Norquist concept of "starving the beast."

The university, which you will recall had not always been popular with the traditionalists, became a target for repeated budget cuts. Adjusting for inflation the university system has been cut by 24.9 percent between FY 2008 and FY 2014. At Chapel Hill, since 2008 they have had to "eliminate 493 positions, cut 16,000 course seats, increased class sizes, cut its centrally supported computer labs from seven to three…" and do other "belt tightening". Even as the economy improves, unlike some states that have increased funding, North Carolina is still providing approximately $3,000 less per student than it did in pre recession. To help balance all this out, North Carolina increased tuition by 34.6 percent (See Center on Budget and Policy

Priorities, May 1, 2014 "Funding Higher Education Below Pre Recession Levels.")

Like the Progress Board, there was another group that measured the state's progress and it was called the Southern Growth Policies Board. Even Repulican Governors Martin and Holshauser had joined, and it had established its offices in the Research Triangle Park. McCrory decided that we no longer needed to share best practices and possibly learn from other southern states on education or anything else. In 2013 Governor McCrory recommended that the Board should shut down and since he was chairman, it did.

Instead of addressing practical areas where help was needed, in a paroxysm of traditionalism, the Republicans went after abortion, voter registrations, and public employees – particularly teachers — environmental regulations, Medicaid, the earned income tax credit and virtually anything associated with Obama, the Democratic Party and in their view, socialism. It was bait and switch; they campaigned on a platform of "jobs, jobs, jobs," but once in power they rewarded their base with demagoguery on social issues. As far as teachers were concerned, they eliminated tenure, removed the bonus for advanced degrees, increased class size, eliminated the Teaching Fellows Program for attracting outstanding students into the profession and, of course, left wages flat. It was a giant leap backward. Once North Carolinians had compared themselves to Virginia or other aspirant states; now we were comparing ourselves to South Carolina or Mississippi.

In January 2013, the new leaders of the Republican General Assembly met with members of the John Locke Foundation and other conservatives to preview the upcoming legislative session. Not surprisingly, the room was suffused with hubris – they were, after all, in a position to dictate whatever policy direction they chose. They chose a radical departure from North Carolina's progressive past. When one of the self-described conservatives left the room, he described the agenda as "breathtaking" and he probably thought it couldn't be done. He was right on the "breathtaking" part and wrong that it couldn't be done.

Shortly after the legislative session opened on January 30, the general tone was set, making it clear that the Redeemers majority was going to enact business-friendly legislation and enforce their federalist concept of states' rights. If they had expressly included white supremacy in their agenda, it might have sounded like something out of 1898. Within weeks they began putting meat on the bones. They charged ahead and dragged the new governor along, sometimes not consulting with him at all. By mid-February, they had passed bills reducing the length of time one could receive unemployment benefits and cutting the amount of those benefits. They also refused to accept extended federal benefits, thus cutting 70,000 people off the unemployment rolls. They then rejected a Medicaid expansion and refused to set up a healthcare insurance exchange as called for under the Affordable Care Act, thus ironically leaving it to the hated federal government to set up the exchange.

The gamble initially spearheaded by Ed Gillespie and Karl Rove and aided and abetted by Art Pope had paid off. And in the policies enacted by the new General Assembly, we have an indication of what to expect from a U.S. Congress run by the Republicans.

OUR MEAN STATE

My own distress about the legislative actions was such that I wrote a piece for *Metro Magazine* in April 2013, titled "Our Mean State:"

I have heard a lot about red states and blue states and a lot about a "nanny state" but not so much about mean states and 'evil stepmother' states. Unfortunately I fear that my beloved adopted state of North Carolina could be characterized by either one or both of these descriptions. By 'mean' I want to imply 'intending to be hurtful' rather than 'stingy,' although that too might apply. By 'evil stepmother' state I'm thinking of Cinderella's stepmother who made her sleep on the floor and eat ashes or something like that.

It was to be expected that these Republicans, who we are constantly reminded were out of power for 140 years, would be intent on putting their own mark on the state. Well, first let me remind you that the Republicans are not the party of Lincoln or even of Theodore Roosevelt. These

Republicans are more akin to Strom Thurmond and as conservative Democrats they ruled the state until WWII. Next, making your own mark doesn't necessarily mean waging a revolution on the poor. But, I'm going to contend that is just what the Republicans in the General Assembly are now doing. In their eagerness to turn back the clock and shrink government they are hurting the most vulnerable of our citizens. I wish I thought this was merely by chance - that the poor were being hit unintentionally - but I'm beginning to think the Republicans' major initiatives are intended to hurt the poor and that's why they strike me as mean spirited.

Let's take a look at the evidence. First, the decision not to take the Medicaid assistance available under Obamacare; By turning down the federal dollars available for expanding our Medicaid rolls they are denying assistance to some 500,000 poor people who would otherwise be eligible to get affordable healthcare. Moreover, it wouldn't cost the state anything - the federal government would pay 100 percent of the cost for three years and 90 percent thereafter. That money will now go to other states and among them are states governed by Republicans, which have decided it's too good a deal to pass up. The only reason our Honorables have given for their action is that they don't think the Feds will actually come through with the funds. So 500,000 of our poorest citizens are denied affordable healthcare because of an unsubstantiated suspicion in Raleigh.

Then there is the decision to turn down federal funds so that benefits could be extended until January 2014 for the long-term unemployment. Affected will be 170,000 people, victims of a stagnant economy. It was all part of North Carolina's unemployment "reform policy" which cut maximum weekly benefits from $535 to $350 – a 35 percent drop; reduced the number of weeks for collecting benefits to between 12 and 20 weeks from 26 weeks, and made qualifying more difficult. While some other southern states have cut unemployment compensation, North Carolina's cuts are the most drastic and this in a state with unemployment over 9 percent so jobs are hard to find.

Next there is the matter of the earned income tax credit (EITC), a program previously supported by Republicans and Democrats, to provide tax relief for the working poor. It gives a tax rebate to working but low-income people to help lift them out of poverty. Last year more than 900,000 working North Carolinians claimed the credit because lots of our citizens are distinctly low income (per capita income $25,256). On 14 March Governor McCrory changed all that by signing the bill that will increase taxes on low and moderate-income people in North Carolina by ending EITC.

Finally, there is the income tax reform currently under consideration. There is no way to tell what the eventual outcome will be, but we do know what the goal is. The Republican objective is to radically reduce, or eliminate the state individual income tax and the corporate income tax. Before you wear yourself out either celebrating or laughing, take the reality check by asking where the funds are going to come from to replace these tax funds that represent 40 percent of the state budget. There is only one possible answer – a consumption tax or "user tax" in addition to a tax on services. These are what are, or should be called, regressive taxes. They fall unequally on the poor. A regressive tax means that "as a household's income rises, even significantly, the tax remains almost the same – the tax burden falls more heavily on households with lower incomes" (Engel's law). To my mind there is no way this can be seen as anything other than a direct assault on the poor.

•••

Governor McCrory has vowed to change North Carolina. It appears that change means taking us back to a time when North Carolina was a low wage state dependent on labor intensive industries and vying with Mississippi for the title of least progressive. As noted by some historians: "The major issue for the state legislature in the 1930s was shifting the tax burden from property and business taxes to the sales tax." (North Carolina History Project) Interestingly the North Carolina History Project is designed and run by the John Locke Foundation. So the Soviets aren't the only ones to see the value in writing your own history.

The General Assembly also indicated their willingness to interfere in local matters, by challenging a deal agreed upon in the last legislative session to convert the Dorothea Dix property in Raleigh into a park. In addition, there was a legislative proposal to transfer ownership and operations of the Charlotte Douglas Airport from the city to a freestanding regional commission and to transfer the Asheville water system from the city to the Metropolitan Sewage District. To the historically minded, this intrusion into local affairs brought memories of the ill-fated efforts in 1893 to exercise more control over county officials. (See p. 34)

The rest of the session is best captured by two articles in Raleigh's *News & Observer* of July 28, 2013. In fact, breathtaking "seems like an understatement," wrote John Frank. "The Republican supermajority, backed by Gov. Pat McCrory, dramatically reshaped the North Carolina landscape, upending decades of settled law, cutting once-sacred institutions and redefining the state's political vision."

That vision will now include laws requiring photo IDs to vote, impose a flat tax, make it more difficult to obtain an abortion, cut unemployment benefits, cut public school appropriations while giving vouchers for private schools, reduce or weaken regulations on businesses, restart executions, weaken gun laws, and outlaw Sharia law in North Carolina. John Hood of the John Locke Foundation noted that "other states have done pieces of this but not all at the same time…" That North Carolina had accomplished all this in one legislation session struck Hood as "phenomenal." It was the conservative Senate that "drove the agenda" wrote Frank. "It crafted a detailed agenda at the start of the session" put it on one page and President Pro Tem Phil Berger "checked them off getting nearly every one."

Naturally, not everyone in the General Assembly was pleased. Representative Darren Jackson, a Democrat, worried that whereas, "North Carolina has had a moderate brand to companies, education, everything"… now with this partisan shift we may well have "a problem when you are trying to attract new businesses, when you are trying to keep the brightest minds in the state."

Rob Christensen, long-time political writer for the *Raleigh N & O* and author of a history of North Carolina politics, titled his editorial "The North Carolina Way Takes a Sharp Right Turn." He called what had happened, "radical surgery in the state's body politic." He cited historian Karl Campbell as saying that North Carolina's self-image as a progressive, moderate state had been "rejected by this legislature." Christensen's view was that "North Carolina has moved from being a regional leader to a follower." He again quotes Campbell as saying, "In this legislature there was not even a pretense of trying to provide political balance."

According to Christensen the deriving intellectual concept was the Republican faith in Reaganomics – the idea that tax cuts brought about economic growth. This, he sees as a "major gamble for the state." He notes that an economist at North Carolina State University found "little evidence that lower state taxes will actually have much of an effect on the state's economic growth."

What the lower taxes will do is hurt North Carolina's school system. Note that the new budget is anticipated to bring in $2.4 billion <u>less</u> over the next five years. Public school funding has fallen from $7.9 billion in 2007-2008 to $7.5 billion during the current year. Given normal growth, the budget should be $9.9 billion this year. The UNC system "long considered the state's crown jewel" endured a budget cut to $2.6 billion whereas again with normal growth it would be $3.7 billion. All of this when North Carolina had never been a high tax state – with a burden of 9.91 percent in 2010 compared to a national average of 9.9 percent. Christensen traces this obsession with the government revenue and hence the size of government back to Jesse Helms who is the "role model" for the current legislature.

At one time, creative southern governors such as William Winter of Mississippi and Bill Clinton of Arkansas "beat a path to North Carolina to learn about the newest policy innovations. Now the conversation in Raleigh has flipped. It is focused on how North Carolina can catch up to its neighbors by having the lowest taxes and the fewest regulations. North Carolina has moved from being a regional leader to a follower."

CHAPTER VI
"ANATOMY OF DISASTER"

What happened to put the current group of legislators in control of the state's political apparatus? Why, after at least fifty years of modernist government under both Democrats and Republicans, was there a radical turn to the right? Let's be clear about one thing – the people in control in Raleigh now are not traditional Republicans, at least in the North Carolina sense. To generalize, one might call them Libertarians or Republican/Libertarians or Tea Party Populists. The moderate voices have been drowned out and control is now in the hands of the more radical element or those who see that element as the base to which they must pander. What this illustrates is that North Carolina's theme of taking at least two steps backward for each step forward. This time the retrogressive forces had to wait in the wings for fifty years, but they waited and patiently plotted their return. When the time came, they out-organized and out-hustled the Democratic Party.

Also of interest is the fact that the Redeemers leadership is made up of people with biographies not seen in North Carolina history since the 1868 "Reconstruction" Constitution was written in part by Carpetbaggers. Governor Pat McCrory was born in Columbus, Ohio, although you won't find that in his internet bio. He went to Catawba College, after which he worked for Duke Power for 28 years. The president pro tem of the N. C. Senate is Phil Berger, who was born in New Rochelle, New York. He went to Averett College, a private liberal arts college in Virginia, and then Wake Forest. The Speaker of the N. C. House is Thom Tillis, who was born in Jacksonville, Florida. Tillis claimed that he graduated from the University of Maryland in College Park, or that is what he originally said, later retracting that and saying he attended Maryland University College, a distance learning college "affiliated" with the university system. Never have the three leaders of a party all been born out of state and rarely has there been no graduate of a UNC institution. It is logical to assume that collectively they might be a little less aware of North Carolina history and traditions and a little less committed to the UNC system.

THE CONTINUING CONSERVATIVE IMPULSE

Traditionalist forces in North Carolina had never really gone away. Every Democratic governor since Luther Hodges, despite their modernist impulses, had to keep an eye out for the white supremacists and the traditionalist business oligarchs. And there were always other candidates who were inclined to go backward, or at least stop going forward very fast, and they could win elections, especially in the East. Jesse Helms is the purest example of a politician who played to the rural, traditionalist voter and who most clearly resembles those now in power in Raleigh. He wasn't alone, though. There was Willis Smith, who defeated Frank Porter Graham, joined by I. Beverly Lake, Lauch Faircloth, John East and, since 1990, Art Pope and the John Locke Foundation. There were two Republican governors in the 20th century, but they were much more moderate, even more liberal, than today's Republicans. The North Carolina House had a Republican majority in 1994 and 1996 and that party has never received less than 40 percent of the vote in every national election since Ronald Reagan in 1980. So in some ways their victory in 2010 was the continuation of a trend.

THE STATE OF THE DEMOCRATIC PARTY

As in every political contest, you have to consider the strength of the opposition. The N.C. Democratic Party slowly began to fall apart in 2000. Jim Hunt's machine had virtually closed down after his first administration, was revived, and then lost cohesion during his second. Unlike political leaders in the past, men like Furnifold Simmons and O. Max Gardner, Hunt did not leave the working political machinery to continue his legacy. During his terms the Democratic Party had been secondary to the Hunt organization in terms of policy and patronage – by the time he left office, the party was a hollow shell. Senator Marc Basnight was the most powerful Democrat in the 21st century. His able assistant was the Senate majority leader, Tony Rand. Together they were a money-raising machine, but in 2009 Rand retired and within the year Basnight became ill. Despite his weakened condition, Basnight did the best he could; but Rand's replacement, Martin Nesbitt, was a mountain populist who lacked the contacts or the associations Rand had, particularly with the business community. The party had election committees run by sitting members of the legislature, but they didn't do much as campaign organizers or as recruiters for new candidates. They did raise some money, but as time went by, it was clear that their campaign more or less ran on automatic. Their complacency was based on the premise that what had worked in the past to win elections would always work.

There wasn't much help in holding the party together from the governor's office. Mike Easley had run as an outsider, not as the anointed successor of Jim Hunt. Thus he destroyed any chances of a Hunt "dynasty" like that of Simmons or Gardner. That might have been fine had he not tarnished himself and the Democratic brand; North Carolina governors – love 'em or hate 'em — had been known for their propriety. Not that there hadn't been a scandal every now and then, but in relation to the government of other states, North Carolina had been a model. Easley was an embarrassment and many Democrats were happy to see him and his wife leave the mansion. Needless to say, his trial in 2009 for misusing campaign funds didn't make fundraising for 2010 any easier.

There also was little help for state legislative candidates from the Democratic National Committee or the Barack Obama political organization. For some odd reason Democrats at the national level relaxed after the 2008 election. Maybe they thought that North Carolina was now a reliably Democratic bastion, an example other southern states might follow. A victory can do curious things to people. The Obama organization had its own, somewhat narrow focus. They wanted to maintain contact with the new voters who had come out in 2008, in order to be ready for 2012. They set up their own independent phone banks, which seldom mentioned candidates for statewide office. Despite receiving repeated pleas, they refused to share their campaign data bank and its list of potential Democratic voters. There was some cooperation between state and presidential campaigns, but not much. At the same time, the presidential campaign team drew away from local races the time and talents of some of the best in-state political volunteers.

THE REDEEMER/ TEA PARTY COALITION

The Republican Party apparatus was a whole different story. Whereas the Democrats were disorganized and leaderless in 2010, the Republicans were energized, organized and focused. Their state party organization got money and advice from the John Locke Foundation and its loyal supporters. Their party chairman was former Raleigh mayor, Tom Fetzer, who ran a well-organized campaign. Talk radio was overwhelmingly supportive and their local affiliates received weekly talking points and fundraising suggestions. But most important was the help provided from the national level by Ed Gillespie and Karl Rove and some other smart operatives who had figured out that on a cost-benefit basis, taking over state legislatures could pay big dividends.

But the Republicans couldn't have done it on their own. In a repeat of what had happened in 1894, the Republicans formed a coalition with the Tea Party, a modern version of the Populist Party. That group, underwritten by conservative super-PACs, was "mad as hell and weren't going to take it anymore." Many of them were working-class people who had been badly stung by the Great Recession. Moreover, their wages had been stagnant since the 1990s and they wanted someone to blame. It wasn't hard for Republican policy wonks to turn their anger on the "government." The government hadn't helped them because it was too busy helping those "other people" – code for African American people. Now, they claimed, we had an illegitimate

African American president who would like to turn the country into Europe! A natural alliance was formed.

THE NATIONAL ECONOMY

In 2010 North Carolina was still suffering from the Great Recession. Although the experts said that the recession had ended in 2009, nobody in North Carolina believed them. For years the state had seen the slow erosion of the textile and furniture industries; tobacco had also been hard hit. Many textile plants had been in small towns in central and eastern parts of the state where they offered low-wage jobs to people with minimum skill levels. In eastern North Carolina, which was a poor region already, the closing of a textile mill was a body blow to the local economy. The furniture industry had been moving overseas for years, but with the collapse of the housing market, things got worse fast. And it was the housing market and its partner, the construction industry, that helped drag the whole state down. Unemployment reached 11 percent, with even retailers laying off workers because of a decline in customers. The service industry struggled as people cut back on discretionary spending like going out to eat. Just as the economic crisis of 1893 brought the Fusionists into power, the Great Recession helped the Republicans

The Great Recession was a shock to the psyche of a large group of North Carolina voters. As has been pointed out, North Carolina had long lagged the national average in per capita income, so North Carolina was particularly vulnerable to economic shocks, but there was another contributing factor to voter anger. Nationally, the middle-class income had been stagnant since 1981, when the average wage earner had brought home $277.35 a week – by 2004 that had grown by only 32 cents to $277.57 (U.S. Bureau of Labor Statistics). While never strong in North Carolina, the power of unions had also diminished during the later part of the 20th century and with them had gone healthcare and other benefits for many workers. By 2010 many voters were angry and frustrated; their homes had gone down in value; their equity lines and their credit cards were tapped out; one or more family members had lost their jobs; and they were looking for somebody to blame. Some of their anger focused on Wall Street and the super rich who, ironically and unbeknownst to them, would pour millions into the next election, though not in support of the party that would help those most damaged. So there was plenty of ire to go around. Stimulated by Glen Beck, Fox News, and the Tea Party, many working-class guys and gals turned their anger on public employees and government in general — "Why should these people have job security and pensions and healthcare, when we don't?" became the refrain. It was classic. Instead of asking why private employers didn't provide them with basic benefits, Tea Partiers turned their anger on those who did receive benefits – it was paycheck envy stimulated by jealousy.

These were hard times to be sure, but the economy offered the Redeemers an attractive target. Through a cleverly orchestrated campaign, they managed to convince gullible voters that the Democratic Party in Raleigh had contributed to, if not caused, the downturn in North Carolina. Obama, they claimed, was responsible for bailing out the banks and Wall Street while neglecting Main Street. And while the public suffered, "government workers" luxuriated in posh jobs. "Jobs" was the answer and the Republicans promised to bring them back. One way, they said, was to get rid of illegal "aliens" who were taking jobs away from Americans. While the Farm Bureau, the construction industry, and others who relied on migrant workers argued for a program for bringing more migrant workers legally into the state, Republican candidates whipped up anti-immigrant sentiment. Crowds at rallies booed the proposed North Carolina version of the federal "Dream Act" which would grant in-state tuition to children of illegal aliens who had come as infants and attended North Carolina schools. All this played well with middle-class, rural voters and the traditionalist base that had always been there.

Full disclosure requires that I reveal that I was the Democratic candidate for the N. C. Senate from North Carolina's 11th District. As a novice, I needed plenty of help and got it from my friends, but there was no help and no money from the Democratic Party. Doubtless, I was inexperienced and may not have run a very good campaign; moreover, I did things like favoring the state's version of the "Dream Act" and was hammered as a result. I also was targeted by the REDSTATE project and was overwhelmed by "dark money" from out of state.

THE TEA PARTY

The Tea Party, which had gained momentum by opposing The Affordable Care Act, had established a firm foothold in the state. Calling themselves Tea Party Patriots, they founded county chapters and staged rallies against our "Socialist" president and "Obamacare." When Democratic congressmen held "listening sessions" with constituents, they were barraged with hostile questions, shouted down, and sometimes forced to cancel appearances. Although clearly local grass-roots organizations, the Tea Partiers were encouraged by and received financial support from out of state. Naturally, they opposed all new taxes and even some already existing ones. Governor Perdue had instituted a .075 percent sales tax to help fund schools, and this became a lightning rod. Although costing the average family less than $12 per month, this levy brought in an estimated $750 million for badly needed aid for public schools. That didn't matter to the Tea Party Patriots – it was a tax and they hated taxes. Jobs, jobs, jobs — that was the answer, and while no one offered a real plan for job creation, it provided a nice refrain. Nor did anyone point out that North Carolina's jobs picture was directly linked to the national jobs picture. Just as they had claimed that the recession was caused by the Democrats at the state level, they now implied that policies enacted by the Redeemers would end the recession. It was an illogical and ridiculously local explanation.

THE LOSS OF THE BUSINESS COMMUNITY

Historically the business community had been an important, or even deciding factor in elections dating from the 19th century. Both parties sought support from the business community, which was pandered to by whichever party was in power. Although you cannot generalize about something as diverse as the "business community," it is the case that since the mid-20th century the largest banks and corporations were, within limits, supportive of forward-looking policies likely to strengthen the state economy. They particularly liked the university system, which provided a talented workforce and whose graduates were seen by many as the "economic engine" of North Carolina.

Business people were also sensitive about maintaining the positive image of the state – they liked slogans like "Dixie Dynamo," "Variety Vacationland" and "First in Flight." They liked hearing North Carolina described as a "progressive southern state" and regular winner of surveys as among the best states in which to do business. A good quality of life — meaning in part, clean air and clean water—attracted talented workers who were in demand and could go anywhere. And those businessmen and their employees wanted good public schools to which they could send their children. So, while it can certainly be said that few of them could be called "liberals" they had, for at least the previous sixty years, favored many aspects of the progressive program. It was, after all, enlightened self-interest. So what happened? Either the business community changed its views, or at least acquiesced in a new approach; or business leaders weren't paying attention, which is a little hard to believe.

Something happened in the early years of the 21st century that changed the attitude of the business community. These were the years of accelerated mergers and acquisitions during which a number of big North Carolina businesses became more national or even international in scope. The process is best illustrated by Wachovia Bank collapsing during the recession and being acquired by Wells Fargo; American Tobacco becoming part of Fortune Brands; and Duke Power becoming a national — rather than a state or regional — company when it became Duke Energy. What this meant was that some of the major corporate players in North Carolina now had less interest in what was going on in the state's politics, even education politics. Moreover, it would appear that they were willing to let low taxes and weak regulations trump public welfare.

Part of the answer may lie in the story of North Carolina Citizens for Business and Industry, or NCCBI. If there ever was an ideal Republican/business supporter/educator, it was Phil Kirk, who headed NCCBI from 1988 – 2005. He'd been a Republican state senator, he was a teacher, and from 1997 - 2003 he was the chairman of the North Carolina State Board of Education. In addition he served on the board of the community college system. When Kirk became head of NCCBI, he quickly moved to bring onto the board educators as well as business leaders. The annual meetings were well-attended by the leading CEOs in the state as well as by elected officials and interested citizens. Kirk made no secret of the fact that he thought a fine education system was essential to business success in the 21st century and he worked eighty hours a week serving the dual masters of business and education. An extremely bright, personable executive, he had seen politics from the inside, having served as a cabinet secretary, as chief of staff under governors Holshouser and Martin, as well as on the staff of Senator James Broyhill. He was by temperament a moderate/progressive although maintaining a strong conservative streak. He was the insiders' insider – trusted by both sides of the political spectrum. But it should be emphasized that with regard to education, Kirk was also acting on the instruction of his board who were themselves very supportive of the public education system in North Carolina.

In 2000, when the University of North Carolina joined with the community college system in seeking $3.2 billion in bonds, Phil Kirk was the logical person to head the drive. Voters overwhelmingly supported the referendum, thus demonstrating the public's commitment to higher education. However, within four years, there began to be rumblings that Kirk was maybe too committed to education issues. The deciding issue seemed to come when Kirk accepted the position of chairman of the State Board of Education. "How," some business executives began to ask, "can he do two full time jobs? We are paying, are we getting our money's worth?" Kirk pushed back, perhaps to the extent of seeming dismissive of the questions. The rumblings grew, abetted by some of Art Pope's supporters who already had questions about the state's educational system.

By 2004 it was clear that Kirk's days at NCCBI were limited. A search committee was formed and they found the candidate they liked in Kansas. Lew Ebert had been head of the Kansas Chamber for three and a half years and had been successful in eliminating the property tax on business equipment and machinery. The primary issues upon which he had focused were healthcare costs, halting lawsuit abuse, reducing taxes on business, lowering unemployment compensation, reducing workers' compensation costs, "all the while leveraging education and transportation investments to grow more Kansas jobs." But when it came to expounding on these issues, the Kansas chamber website made no mention of education. The new head of NCCBI would not be running the risk Kirk had of spending too much time on education issues; lowering business costs and getting rid of troublesome regulations would be where Ebert would focus. If we can understand why the folks running the NCCBI – soon to be the N. C. Chamber – changed from supporting Phil Kirk to supporting Lew Ebert, we will have a better perspective of what changed within the business community.

Some would suggest that the whole modus operandi and horizons of the business community had changed or were changing in the early years of the 21st century. Instead of a twenty-year vision, banks and other financial institutions were thinking more in terms of five years. Compensation and promotion were more and more closely tied to the bottom line. One big investor told me that long-time associations and loyalty counted for less and less. If time horizons have shrunk, then education, which is a long-term investment, would have less appeal.

Then, after 2007 there was the recession, which hammered North Carolina businesses. Soon the state had the dubious distinction of being among the leaders in unemployment. Stockholders logically insisted that the focus should be strictly on regaining profitability. It could be reasonably argued that education was not their highest priority.

Finally, by 2010, the "Grand Bargain" at the national level had been badly eroded. (See p. 42) The regulations and the safety net that had "shaped the contours of U.S. political and economic life between 1940 and 2000... had been under attack from conservatives for decades." Some could argue that Clinton's triangulation, or finding middle ground, cut the legs out from under a liberal agenda. But whatever the reasons, the structure of the bargain no longer held, and Obamacare, part of the grand tradition of protecting people from the vagaries of the insurance and pharmaceutical market, was a bridge too far. Labor unions were declining in power, Glass-Steagall had been repealed, the minimum wage remained at 1970 levels, and regulatory commissions were underfunded. From this perspective, North Carolina was part of a general retrograde movement. We just happened to be easier to move because of our long and long-disguised traditionalist impulse. In this case the tradition was founded in the 1890s during the Gilded Age.

The modern blueprint for this change had been laid years before. In 1971 Lewis Powell, later a Supreme Court Justice, had written an extraordinary memorandum to the Chamber of Commerce. He titled it "A Call to Arms," in which he summoned the Chamber to become more actively involved in politics in order to block the "assault" on the free enterprise system. In it he cautioned, in language one associates more with the John Birch Society than with a jurist, that the "American economic system is under attack." He pinned the blame on academics and a liberal media who were aiding and abetting Socialists, Communists and Fascists. Our country was a risk and the Chamber and its business associates needed to save it by establishing think tanks, speaker's bureaus and its own groups of influence-makers to balance those on the left. And he reminded the Chamber of the power of the judiciary, "American business and the enterprise system have been affected as much by the courts as by the executive and legislative branches of government. Under our constitutional system, especially with an activist-minded supreme court, the judiciary may be the most important instrument for social, economic and political change." In essence he called for repeal of the Grand Bargain, since he saw business getting the worst of the deal. Out of his memorandum grew the Heritage Foundation and ALEC among other initiatives (see Appendix).

His comments about the courts helped fuel support for a more right-leaning judicial system. Powell, himself, became a justice in 1971 and by the 1980s the Supreme Court became distinctly more conservative and pro business. By 2000 that Court helped elect a Republican president. In 2010 they handed down Citizens United and in 2014 it was McCutcheon v. Federal Elections Commission, both decisions that helped business owners, the wealthy, and the Republican Party, which joined in bringing McCutcheon to the Supreme Court.

What does this have to do with the Grand Bargain and North Carolina? It is only speculation, but not unreasonable to think that business became less fearful of legal intervention and enforcement of rules and regulations once they had courts that were likely to rule in their favor. The Grand Bargain only held when it was backed up by the muscle of the federal government. This also helps explain the generalized attack on "government" led by the Koch brothers and other business owners who resent interference in their "free enterprise" activities. The North Carolina connection became clearer to me when I learned that more than $800,000 came in to North Carolina in 2012 to influence the election of a justice to the North Carolina State Supreme Court. Why would out-of-state interests care that much about a state court? Because they recognized that courts, as Lewis Powell said, "may be the most important instrument for social, economic and political change." Moreover, they might have noticed that one federal prosecutor appointed by George W. Bush had successfully prosecuted a North Carolina governor, congressman, speaker of the House and a U.S. senator – all Democrats. No doubt they were all guilty, but it was quite an assault on one party at a time when power was relatively equally divided. Interestingly, that prosecutor successfully ran for Congress on the Republican ticket in 2012.

The change in the attitude of the business community was welcomed by the people at the John Locke Foundation and others for whom public education had always been suspect or of secondary importance. Indeed, for years there had been, in some quarters, outright opposition to the principle of public education. Based in part on the proposition that public schools were failing, the call was to close so-called "government-run schools" and allow the free market to provide education. This has special appeal to Libertarians and people like Bob Luddy, who runs a group of for-profit schools in the Raleigh area and is Art Pope's Civitas board chairman. He had published a pamphlet titled "The Path to Prosperity: Spending Cuts, No Income Tax and Free Market Schools." As this clearly indicates, for some, support for private schools may have more to do with the money that can be made in the education business than with the ideology of free enterprise.

Recent scholarship would suggest yet another factor concerning the business community. While it had been assumed that Citizens United would open the floodgates of corporate money, that isn't exactly what happened. Corporate contributors to the Republican Party and to certain candidates did go up, but not as fast as the money contributed by extremely wealthy individuals. Their money swamped that of corporations. In 2012 the top 0.1 percent of donors contributed more than 44 percent of all campaign contributions; in 1980 their share of contributions had been less than 10 percent (*NY Times* "Business Losing Clout in a GOP Moving Right" September 3, 2012). The article concludes, "If big money people are drowning out the political voice of Americans rather than big business, American Democracy still has a problem. But it is not the problem we thought we had." In North Carolina the big ideological givers were the Koch brothers and North Carolina's Art Pope.

BARACK HUSSEIN OBAMA

When he squeaked to victory in North Carolina in 2008, Barack Obama brought what proved to be unfortunate attention to the state. While Democrats celebrated the change of North Carolina from red to blue, his victory steeled Republican resolve to retake a state they had so narrowly lost. That might have happened under any conditions, but the fact that Obama was black was particularly helpful. There had always been more than a touch of racism in the state; it was there in 1898 and it was there to help elect Jesse

Helms to five terms. It was also there in the Smith-Graham contest; it was there in the KKK numbers in the 1960s; it was always there just beneath the surface. Even in the Hunt elections he got the votes of those called Jessecrats, registered Democrats who voted for Jesse in national elections, in part, because Jesse opposed civil rights legislation. Jim Hunt was okay because, while a modernizer and not a racist, he was a good Christian boy with a rural background who had gone to N. C. State.

But in the early 21st century, racism assumed an even more ominous character. Demographic studies showed that the racial composition of the country and the state was changing. Now, demographers and journalists could tell you that in the 21st century, the U.S. would become more black and brown than white. That's right, white people would become the minority. Those paying attention knew that North Carolina was seeing one of the fastest growing Hispanic populations in the country. When those people, with their high birth rate, joined the blacks, they could run the state. Moreover, there were other dire changes evident. Now we had female justices on the U.S. Supreme Court and one of them was named Sotomayor. Then gays wanted to get married and, incredibly, there were gays in the military. For many people, particularly in rural parts of the state, their worst nightmares were coming true. These fears helped to fire the Redeemers uprising.

PUBLIC EDUCATION

Public education and the taxes to support it had often been an issue in North Carolina politics. In 2010 and 2012 traditionalist candidates tied support for public education to government in an obvious attempt to link public schools to the much maligned, intrusive, "government." But there were also larger issues involved, which provided attractive targets for naysayers. The performance of K-12 schools had long been a matter of broad concern. There were many critics of the schools, particularly in light of poor U.S. performance on international tests as compared to other countries. Unquestionably, we were doing poorly in regard to sciences and math, and many schools in inner cities and poor rural areas were struggling to pass even the relatively easy state-mandated tests. No one could agree on a solution; some wanted more testing, some wanted smaller classes, and some wanted less testing. There was general agreement that good teachers were essential, and since 1990 there had been an effort to improve teacher pay, to at least get it to the national average. But even with incentives, we continued to have high turnover. An effort was made to improve the quality of principals by establishing principals' academies on grounds that good principals could improve discipline and provide teacher support. To improve the quality of teachers there were special scholarships like the Teaching Fellows Program for those students intending to go into the profession. But to many it appeared like a "solution of the year" situation, with everyone, including teachers, being pulled first one way and then another.

A lightning rod was the school board war in Wake County. In the 2009 school board election a familiar group of characters poured money into the campaigns of traditionalist candidates in Wake, the 18th largest school district in the country. The Koch brothers and their organization, Americans for Prosperity, provided funding for Tea Party activists to put up a slate of conservative candidates. Who would have thought that the Koch brothers – of New York and Kansas — would have chosen to fund an off-year school board election in North Carolina?

The answer may be tied to Art Pope's membership on the board of Americans for Prosperity. What we do know is that Pope himself gave $15,000 to the Wake County GOP to support conservative school board candidates. The primary issue was opposition to the policy of integrating schools based on income. Under this program, no more than 40 percent of the students in any school could be receiving subsidized lunches, an indication of poverty. It was an innovative and nationally recognized way of getting away from integrating schools solely on race while still insuring diversity. "Neighborhood schools" was the mantra of the conservatives; and they won, thus setting off a battle between traditionalists and modernizers. Another thing the Wake race surely did was give opponents of public schools an example of what they portrayed as liberals run rampant in search of diversity. One wonders if the integration issue will ever go away in North Carolina.

There also were those who had complaints about the university system. George Leef and others at the Pope Center for Higher Education Policy had long been critics of the UNC university system, its curriculum, and the quality of its graduates. The Pope Center was actually the John William Pope Center, named for Art's father who, along with Jesse Helms, had seen the University at Chapel Hill as a hotbed of liberals and gays. For Helms, opposing UNC was all part of an anti-intellectual bias, which appealed to his more conservative listeners on WRAL. Integration of the university was more grist for their mill. Leef insists that he is not really a conservative critic of higher education, just a critic of certain aspects of higher education. He writes that the Pope Center is not against all college education. It wants only to "trim and redirect funding for it, reform policies of it and improve its ideological climate." Exactly what he means by "ideological climate" is not explicit, but from his other writings we know that he thinks universities have watered down their requirements, spent too much time on African or other non-western history and offered too many courses on the gay lifestyle. He very specifically believes that the universities' schools of education are dominated by liberal professors who teach left-wing theories. "The trouble," he says, "is that those theories do not help train teachers to instruct their students as best as possible." He adds, disingenuously, "Anyone who looks objectively at the work of the Pope Center will find that we are only interested in constructive criticism of higher education in America."

There are grounds for criticizing higher education, including its cost and its drift away from a traditional curriculum. But the idea that Chapel Hill and the other UNC schools are dominated by left-wing professors ignores the fact that most students are not majoring in history, political science, sociology or other social sciences. Most are majoring in business, computer science, criminal justice or physical education, etc. Very few professors could find a way to inject ideology into those courses, much less into courses in math and the other sciences. The point is that while there are liberal professors at public institutions of higher education, there are also conservatives, and if you want to find them, start with the business schools.

Where Leef is closer to the truth is in criticizing the schools of education. Robert E. Tyndall, former dean of the Watson School of Education at UNCW and national consultant on education matters recognizes the problem and points out examples of the type of change needed. "Few subjects ignite passion as does the issue of school support. It was inevitable that those concerned about the inadequacy of schools would eventually expand their criticism to the institutions of higher education where educators are prepared...." Rebuilding public trust, he argues, requires that schools of education see that their most important work is not on the college campus, "but in the classrooms where their graduates practice their craft." Schools of education must share accountability for performance of public school students. "Some programs have acknowledged this linkage and shared responsibility, but the vast majority continues to offer topical courses that often reflect popular movements of the day rather than balancing their curriculums with validated, best practices in reading, math, science or historical analysis that will matter in the school classroom and life."

He points out some changes made by schools leading in this effort:

• Uniformly rigorous admission requirements that include screening applicants on the basis of academic performance including baseline GPA requirements in basic studies, success on a battery of national exams focusing on general knowledge and specialty area content knowledge normed in the top performance quartile, and specified exit examinations/demonstrations focusing on content, pedagogy and technology.

• Real double major requirements that ensure discipline-specific content mastery along with methodology and pedagogical preparation to dispel the "academic weak sister" image of schools of education.

• Establishing a campus Office of Service to Public Schools focusing the resources of the entire campus on school assistance as well as developing a special plan to support designated low-performing districts. This includes aggressive and creative recruitment and financial support for low income and underrepresented populations.

• Creating regional education consortia designed to combine the talents, energy and resources of public schools, community colleges, businesses and the university. Such collaboration has led to a number of nationally recognized school improvement initiatives. Many of the consortia begun in prior decades failed to focus on important work, did not negotiate true partner relations that encouraged mutual assessment, joint funding, leveraged purchasing power or joint appointments. These solutions are needed now more than ever. These partnerships require high levels of commitment and even some of the most successful models faded as leadership changed or objectives became less focused.

• Produce both faculty assistance directories and reciprocal public school faculty assistance directories that outline individual expertise and describe how to access support and actively make the connections happen. Public schools can provide invaluable expertise to universities and can help create integrated work models. Both entities have much to offer, but in most cases the colleges and universities host events and create academic programs in insular environments rather than creating functional work teams. Together we need to heed Phil Schletchty's advice and get busy "working on the work that matters."

• Create comprehensive technology initiatives to ensure that all graduates of educator preparation programs have mastered "essential technology skills" and can demonstrate such mastery. Further, Regional Educational Consortia can assist practicing educators in public schools by offering a host of technology outreach initiatives.

Tyndall also sees much work to be done linking online teaching for teachers and administrators to results in the schools. The list of tasks he names includes establishing science and math education centers on both campuses and public schools. "Results include summer venture programs that provide advanced institutes for interested and academically able high school students, teacher renewal programs, and classroom-based research projects." Ease of transfer from high school to community college to university should be improved by agreements between schools on course content, credits, etc. "These agreements along with new off-campus degree programs and weekend colleges are examples of innovative ways schools of education can join hands in their regions to benefit from collaboration and educational cooperation." Establishing clinical teaching programs in the schools involving public school faculty would help to integrate the levels of schooling and make the education of teachers more real-world classroom-based.

When schools of education immerse themselves in the work of schools and initiate efforts like some of those described above, then important results can be realized. These initiatives are pieces of the puzzle of school improvement. With a broader understanding of the unique roles of colleges and universities in the overall effort and increased understanding of the complexities of the problems, we can recover the central place of education in North Carolina's future. Schools of education need to talk less, listen more, live and breathe the linking of their work to student learning in schools, and engage every citizen in this critical conversation. (Read Tyndall's full critique in the Appendix.)

I strongly agree that schools of education have work to do to be more effective and to regain stronger public trust.

Higher education in the state has not been without its political problems. North Carolina State University did higher education no favors when they offered Mary Easley a job during Governor Easley's second administration. It may be that they didn't exactly offer her a job, rather that they accepted her offer of availability. In any case they compounded the mistake by providing her an inordinately high salary for the position. This caught the attention of the John Locke Foundation which passed it on to Raleigh's *News & Observer* and led to a series of articles, which in turn led to the resignation of the provost and the chancellor.

Then in July 2010 a story broke on academic corruption at the flagship, Chapel Hill. It seemed that some athletes were taking courses for which no actual attendance was required. Moreover, these athletes were getting very good grades for what looked like very little effort. This really hurt; Chapel Hill was supposed to be a model of how to have a winning athletic program *and* a sterling academic reputation. Chapel Hill was an example of the "Carolina Way." To make matters worse, the offending courses were offered in the African American Studies department, which played directly into the hands of traditionalists at the John Pope Center. In any case, there was an NCAA investigation, the stigma of which led to the resignation of the chancellor in 2013.

As with the Democratic Party's ineptitude contributing to the Republican takeover, a similar case can be made regarding the state's mainstream education groups. These organizations had withstood many efforts in the past to derail school improvement, but this time, rather than adopting a unified stance, they splintered and each pursued its chosen goals independently.

Simply stated, there was little leadership provided from within the five organizations that had previously been associated with public school advocacy. Of the five most influential over the last few years was the North Carolina Association of Educators (NCAE), the North Carolina affiliate of the National Education Association (NEA). To the Tea Partiers, the NCAE was a union. They targeted anything resembling a union; and what could be worse than a "government" union? In truth, the NCAE had a well-funded and well-organized political action committee that had historically supported Democratic candidates because those had been the candidates who supported school improvement. Among those improvements was a strong push to raise teacher salaries to the national average. When the political shift occurred in the General Assembly in 2010, the NCAE found itself fighting

Redeemers-sponsored legislation to keep school systems from allowing deduction of dues from members' salaries. By 2013 there had been a large drop in membership, causing financial strain and philosophical differences to surface. Faced now with a Redeemer in the mansion, the NCAE decided to play down their public school advocacy function in the 2013 legislative session, hoping perhaps they would thereby avoid unwelcome attention.

Two other statewide organizations, the PTA and the Public School Forum, a non-profit education support group, received state funding that was now at risk. The PTA received $300,000 per year to be used for building stronger local PTA chapters. While not a large amount, it was vital to an organization already underfunded. The Forum was intent on continuing the Teaching Fellows Scholarship Program, which it had conceived in 1987 and administered since its inception. This program had achieved positive results over the years and was seen as a model by other states, which copied it. Again, there was not much money involved, but it was clear that Art Pope, the governor's budget director, was on the hunt for any money-saving ideas.

The Forum and the PTA adopted the same strategy as the NCAE had – keep your head down and maybe you won't be noticed. For whatever reason, both organizations were uncharacteristically quiet. The Forum's email newsletter went for months without even critically mentioning the wrecking ball the General Assembly was swinging through three decades of education improvement efforts. Sometimes silence isn't golden.

The fourth major group that had been in the business of education reform was the School Boards Association, which also decided to keep their heads down and mouths shut. Their top and only funding priority was the elimination of the annual $300 million "discretionary" cuts required by the General Assembly. This clever trick had handed the school boards the dirty work of making unpopular cuts each year of $300 million so that they, rather than the legislators, would get the blame. In order to get rid of this unpopular requirement, the School Boards Association cut themselves loose from the other educational advocacy groups and their support for the NCAE's teacher salary issue, the Forum's effort to save the Teaching Fellows and the

PTA's local project money. It reminds one of those survivors in a lifeboat story which comes down to every man for himself. It must have cheered their opponents to see the educational groups losing all cohesion.

The last major educational group in the state is the North Carolina Association of School Administrators, an overarching organization including superintendents, principals, finance officers, curriculum specialists and others. Though technically independent, their position on issues usually reflected that of the School Boards Association since their members work in local school districts overseen by school boards.

So, all five major groups took a narrow, non-collaborative approach, something approximating a defensive crouch. Interestingly, this unattractive posture was chosen by each group independently without consultation. This approach was the absolute opposite to that which had been taken when public school improvement previously was the agenda. In those years, collaboration and cooperation had been the watchwords not only within the educational community, but the business community as well. For a decade three of the groups – the School Associations, the administrators and the Public School Forum – formed the "Education: Everybody's Business Coalition" which worked for school improvement. They, in company with NCCBI (the predecessor of the North Carolina Chamber) worked closely with the General Assembly and the governor's office on projects intended to improve public schools. They met monthly, adopted a common legislative agenda and lobbied as one. It was the common effort that helped pass the record bond issues. When, after 2006, NCCBI mutated into the North Carolina Chamber, out went the common agenda and the education coalition. The Chamber thereafter focused on low taxes and deregulation.

At approximately the same time came another big change that further separated these organizations. The Public School Forum had for years functioned as a meeting point for all groups involved with public education: K-12, the UNC system, the community colleges and the five mainstream organizations already mentioned. This meeting place, although there wasn't always agreement on priorities, did allow opportunity for discussion and collaboration. For years the different groups were able to see that the advancement of some issues served everyone's interests. There is, after all, a symbiotic relationship between the schools as students pass from one system to another and then into the workforce. However, in 2013 the Public School Forum changed its bylaws, eliminating this connection with the mainstream groups and the leaders of the three state educational systems. No longer is there a consistent point of contact or a place to form a common agenda.

In the 1990s that common agenda had often defeated efforts to weaken public schools by way of a voucher system that would allow parents to opt out in favor of private schools. A coalition of over fifty educational advocates was quickly put together to lobby against the voucher program. The coalition effectively ended the voucher debate for a decade. Compare that with 2013, when there was no concerted effort to block similar legislation. News stories featured advocates of vouchers, who lauded the concept of allowing parents to choose their students' schools. Like "neighborhood schools" a few years before, vouchers became the epitome of a free market system. Without organized opposition, the voucher bill passed, making North Carolina one of a handful of states passing into law one of the long-held dreams of conservative opponents of public schools.

So, how did the "every man for himself" strategy work out for public education? NCAE saw teachers lose tenure, lose incentive pay for master's degrees and have their salaries frozen for another year. Of course, the General Assembly could have increased teacher salaries had they not eliminated the small sales tax instituted by Governor Perdue and given the wealthiest citizens a big tax cut. But it is easier to deny raises when you have less money available. NCAE saw thousands of teacher and teacher-assistant positions eliminated. The PTA and the Forum lost their funding for local PTAs and the Teaching Fellows Program. The School Boards Association may have come out the best if you like pyrrhic victories. They hadn't liked having to make those $300 million yearly "discretionary" cuts – so, the General Assembly bit the bullet, making the cuts permanent, thereby saving the Schools Boards Association the pain, but at the cost of thousands of positions and support programs. It seems to me that we ought to rethink this. The point is that between 2009 and 2013 the public education system was doing itself no good. It was in this same timeframe that people of all political persuasions began to talk more about charter schools and to praise the technical education provided by the community colleges. It also became popular to question the whole notion of going to college. The conservative former Secretary of Education William Bennett published a book titled *Is College Worth It?,* which he naturally answered in the negative. With tuition continuing to go up, it seemed to many that at some point, and preferably pretty soon, everyone would have to have to answer that college was not worth *that* much.

REPUTATION

In a perverse way the history and reputation of the state could be perceived inaccurately from two opposing points of view. An observer could look at the history and say that North Carolina moved very quickly and very positively during the last sixty years. From this perspective North Carolina was firmly established as one of the up-and-coming states in the country and surely one of the most progressive in the South. North Carolina was clearly a model of the New South, with that reputation hard sought and won. Since that was the case, there was little or no chance the state would choose to move backward. However, this notion of progress could breed complacency. From the opposite point of view, those sixty years of progressive movement were quite enough. The state had gone too far and too fast to the left. Those observers could see the state becoming not only blue, but an example of everything they fretted about – it was becoming liberal, urban, diverse, and too much like New York and California. Moreover, all that progress had cost money. As candidate McCrory said, the state was "broke" and he aimed to fix it. Furthermore, those who held the negative view of the state's direction knew that there was a solid conservative base to which they could appeal. Of course, the state wasn't "broke" as its Constitution required a balanced budget, but that didn't matter, it was a memorable phrase.

As historians and political scientists will tell you, perception is reality.

But in this case both perceptions were wrong. As the Progress Board report showed, North Carolina was for those six decades firmly placed in the middle of America. It was in the top ten in only a very few areas and in the lower twenty in too many others. To use an apt title from a report by the Southern Growth Policies Board, North Carolina was "halfway home with a long way to go." There remained much work to do before we achieved our goals, and retrogressive movement was going to prove to be far too easy. So, North Carolina was neither a liberal state run amok nor a "broken" state in need of a radical makeover.

So when one looks back at what happened, a whole series of causes – some related and some independent – led to the Redeemers takeover. To summarize, they were, in no rank order: the continuing traditionalist strain; the complacent Democratic Party; the Redeemers well-oiled, coordinated organization; out-of-state dark money; the Tea Party; the economy; the loss of business support for progressive policies; Obama; scandals and lack of organization by public education leaders; and finally, the concept that it couldn't happen here. When you put them all together, it is easy to understand how the battle was lost.

CHAPTER VII
WHAT MUST BE DONE

If history is to be of value we might start by restating the themes that have marked our past.

•We have followed a pattern of one step forward, two steps back. Modernizing tendencies have always faced resistance and that resistance has taken the form of revisiting our worst policies and displaying our worst instincts, including racism, anti-intellectualism, misogyny and xenophobia.

• At various points in our history we have turned to voter suppression; using land holding, race, or gender, the traditionalists have sought to limit the vote.

• As the foregoing implies, there has always been a strong conservative strain in North Carolina; even progressive leaders have had to guard against going too far too fast.

• The power of the business community. Although they have varied over time from large landowners to industrialists to bankers to insurance magnates, they have had a disproportionate influence on North Carolina's direction.

• The role of education. Modernizers always saw public education as a democratizing essential and an economic energizer. Traditionalists have been less supportive. They equate education with elitism and see it as giving legitimacy to radical ideas.

• Low taxes have often been the tool to limit educational opportunity <u>and</u> appeal to the business community.

• North Carolina has seen a succession of political dynasties. These dynasties were led by powerful individuals followed by their acolytes. This has been true from Zebulon Vance to Jesse Helms. Jim Hunt's dynasty was a machine that simply ran out of steam when he was no longer running.

• Coalitions. To overthrow the political party in power, it has been necessary to form coalitions. The current coup occurred when the traditional Republicans formed a coalition with the Tea Party.

What can we do to bring North Carolina back to its cherished position as a leader in the South and the nation? Let me be clear that I don't necessarily mean bringing back a Democratic majority – those of us who love the state and are concerned about its future would settle for any party or coalition with an enlightened program for advancement. We are convinced that there are many Holshouser Republicans in North Carolina who must be ashamed of what the Redeemers are doing. And there are the 32 percent of voters registered as independents or unaffiliated, who presumably remain to be convinced that forward is better than backward. The focus of the effort to take the state back from the Tea Party must <u>first</u> be on the Democrats, as candidates who at least have a track record in creating progress, but they can't be the only candidates. People running for office who might be willing to form a <u>coalition</u> with the Democrats would be welcome. Such coalitions have won in the past. The program must be wide-ranging, because the loss of momentum has been so stunning. So what are the elements of a plan needed to turn the state in a more positive direction?

One thoughtful critic had this to say:

"The people of North Carolina no longer trust either party, Democrat or Republican, and also do not trust government to act on their behalf. They see government, state and federal, as serving the moneyed special interest groups as the middle class sees its chances of realizing the American dream dissipate.

In the recent article in the *NY Times* on American the Shrunken, Frank Bruni was quoted as saying, "that the middle class in America, which long has been the world's most affluent, wasn't anymore." Canada had overtaken us. He cites the USA's ranking on a recent social progress index that includes 132 countries. " We're 39th in basic education, 34th in access to water and sanitation and 16th overall."

My sense is that if the South were ranked on that index, even North Carolina would not show up well. So what is the plan for the modernist to change our relative ranking within the U.S. and the world?

I have concluded that the reins of power in the governor's office and the legislature will not be returned to the modernist solely because of the retrograde behavior of the traditionalist. Putting North Carolina back on track to world competitiveness will take a "bold new vision" that contains both facing the brutal facts and pragmatic solutions to issues that are relevant to the long and short term wellbeing of all of the citizens of the state.

North Carolina is a moderate state with progressive leanings based on conservative values.

The people of North Carolina do not want more or less government, they want more <u>effective, accountable</u> government that is <u>fairly paid for</u>, and <u>fairly administered</u>.

They seek a qualified, pragmatic leader with a clear, fact-based understanding of this state's strengths and weaknesses; a genuine concern for the long-term wellbeing of all of the citizens of this state; and a sense of accountability and fiscal responsibility. They want him/her to be knowledgeable about North Carolina's past but not bound by it, electable and trained in the art of governing, desirous of governing, and willing to make the tough decisions that will be called for.

What it needs as its next governor is a pragmatic/progressive who is trained and equipped to govern from day one and surrounds himself/herself with qualified professionals and not political hangers-on."

THE BUSINESS COMMUNITY

If history is any guide, the business community must be won over by the reformers. The change in the national reputation of the state should be a wake-up call for enlightened business interests. Stories in newspapers from New York to Los Angeles are noting that North Carolina is now the "new Mississippi." An editorial in *The New York Times* was particularly damning, stating that since the election of Governor McCrory, "State government has begun a demolition derby, tearing down years of progress in public education, tax policy, racial equality in the court room and access to the ballot." They went on to say, "North Carolina was once considered a beacon of far-sightedness in the South, an exception in a region of poor education, intolerance and tight fistedness. In a few short months, Republicans have begun to dismantle a reputation that took years to build." (See the 9 July 2013, *NY Times* editorial) Rachel Maddow devoted a full hour of airtime on MSNBC to North Carolina's new voting rules. Bill Moyers produced a documentary titled "State of Conflict: North Carolina." In it he points out how far-right Republicans have slashed taxes on the wealthy and corporations, provided school vouchers and rolled back voting rights.

This is not good publicity, nor is it the kind of thing that attracts high-wage industry to your state. Former Secretary of State Colin Powell told a group at a CEO forum in Raleigh, with Governor McCrory in the audience, that the new voting law "turns off a voting bloc the Republican Party needs." He went on to say, "These kinds of actions do not build on the base. It just turns people away...I want to see policies that encourage every American to vote, not to make it more difficult to vote." He might have added that such laws turn businesses away as well. This kind of national publicity surely can't be the kind of rebranding that we really want for the future good of our state.

These actions could turn away the kind of businesses and jobs that we previously have wanted. Industries with low-wage jobs, the equivalent of the old textile and tobacco jobs, may flock to the state. The call centers, the discount stores, the waste disposal groups wanting to dot the state with land-fills or otherwise take advantage of our weakened environmental rules — they may come, but do we want them? My answer is, no. We want the higher-wage, higher-tech jobs that will be part of the knowledge economy.

To get those jobs, we need to improve our reputation and convince our existing business community that the course we are on is not in their best long-term economic interest. There are still many forward-looking business people like Jim Goodman and Jim Goodnight who should form the core of our effort to convince the city executives and other North Carolina-based business people that we are on the wrong track. To do this is going to take effort and organizational skill. If what has happened has happened because the business community was not paying attention or not considering the consequences, they must receive a clear wake-up call from the more enlight-ened and informed among them. In addition, there must be an effort to re-organize and reenergize the business community collectively.

And here let me issue a cautionary note that applies in the case of re-gaining the support of business, as well as with the reforms to be suggested. The urge to bring about change must be focused. Too often in cases such as this, a proliferation of reform efforts can occur that actually impedes the changes being sought. Modernizers, because they believe in the marketplace of ideas, are particularly prone to this fault. The reactionary groups that en-gineered the regressive change we are experiencing are focused and disci-plined – our reform efforts must take a page from their book. If one reform effort is good, three are not necessarily better.

So what is to be done about changing the course of, or awakening, the business community? One possibility would be to reform the current Cham-ber from within. If, as I have suggested, Lew Ebert was brought to the Chamber by a group who wanted to see an agenda adopted that downplayed education and instead emphasized lowering taxes and weakening regulations, a new group needs to take control. Since new private sector CEOs who have supported education in the past are in line to assume the presidency of the Chamber over the next several years, there may well be hope of this change from within.

As has already been mentioned, it may just be that the entire philosophical attitude of the North Carolina business community has changed. They may no longer agree on the principles of the Grand Bargain. They may no longer agree on the positive role of government in people's lives. They may no longer agree that in order for capitalism to remain, it must accept regulation. They may no longer agree that a government-sponsored safety net is needed to protect individuals from fluctuations of the market and what have been called "The four horsemen of accident, illness, old age and joblessness." (E.J. Dionne, *Washington Post,* 23 March, 2014) This debate over the role of government and the obligations of business and the resulting political structure is going on nationally, and as with some other issues; North Carolina may be a test bed among competing ideas.

There also is the possibility of putting together a new group of business leaders who value education and the state's reputation. This new group would be outside the Chamber and free to raise money and support modernizer candidates. At the very least, they would demonstrate that the business community is not monolithic and united in their support for regressive policies. This could take the form of a new Chamber, separate and distinct from the current one, perhaps in the form of a new NCCBI. This would take effort and would require a whole new organizational structure, but it would also send a message that North Carolina was not complacently going backward.

Thankfully there has been movement on this front. A new organization, Business for Education Success and Transformation North Carolina, or BEST NC, has been formed and joined by some of the leading CEOs in the state. The group includes Jim Goodmon, CEO of Capitol Broadcasting; Vanessa Harrison, president of AT&T; Ann Goodnight of SAS; Brad Wilson, CEO of Blue Cross and Blue Shield of North Carolina; and, interestingly enough, Phil Kirk, former head of NCCBI. Walter McDowell, a retired Wachovia executive, is chairman of the group, which, he says, will advocate solutions for better outcomes from preschool to post-secondary education. He goes on to say, "We think that stronger public education outcomes will accelerate job growth and spur economic development." Ann Goodnight, a Republican, specifically attacked the Republican-led General Assembly. "We are under-investing in our pre-K-12, community colleges and university students, and in our teachers. This budget is an embarrassment in its lack of investment in the skills and competitiveness of its people. This is a grievous mistake." (*Raleigh News & Observer*, July 2013)

She is obviously correct, but it remains to be seen what will be done. One discouraging note was struck by some of its leaders, who said that, "BEST NC was not an effort to push back on the reforms enacted in the legislature." Walter McDowell added that, "We do not believe throwing a lot of money at public education is the answer." The "reforms enacted by the legislature?" How are we to get teachers' pay increased without "throwing" some more money into the budget? Moreover, I'm not sure what solutions there are out there that will insure "better outcomes." It is not as though public school educators haven't been seeking better outcomes. But after that is said, it is very welcome to see business leaders acknowledging the importance of education.

Jim Goodnight, Ann's husband and CEO of SAS, in a recent op-ed came out specifically in favor of the common core educational standards noting that he saw "this as an economic issue, because the quality of our graduates directly affects our state's economic well being." He added, "NC businesses have always relied on a strong education system." (*Raleigh News & Observer*, 2 May 2014). While their reliance was backed up with political muscle prior to 2010, what happened to it in the last few years? It is obvious that some CEOs are beginning to see the connection between their influence and the rightward shift.

PUBLIC EDUCATION

It is encouraging to see that some business people are starting to rediscover the connection between education and the economy, but public school supporters must better organize and reform themselves.

Whatever course reformers choose, support for education must be a central driving principle behind any political renaissance. And here, too, there must be a disciplined focus. There are some who want to direct their efforts toward support for the university system, others who want to emphasize K-12, while still others want to support the community college system. Three groups are not better than one. Education, all education, should be the objective and a seamless connection should be the goal.

From the beginning it should be recognized that the three systems — K-12, university and community college — have not always played well together and it would be naïve to assume that they would now. Part of the problem is structural; education funding is a very large part of the general fund budget, and these essential elements of the education system are in a shark tank with each other. After saying that, it may be that the current crisis is of such magnitude that all can see that no one's interest is served by infighting. So, insofar as possible, the three groups should work cooperatively for the common good. As Benjamin Franklin once said, "We must all hang together or assuredly we shall all hang separately." The old Public School Forum, before the bylaws were changed, could serve as a model.

There also must be a common willingness to admit the need for improvement in the way education is delivered. There is no space here to discuss all the possible reforms that could and possibly need to be made. So permit me to sum up: at all levels educators could do a better job. We need to get our graduation levels up; we need to improve access by controlling costs; we need to turn out graduates who are educable; we need to turn out teachers ready to command a classroom and teach. In other words, we can't act as though all of the criticism leveled at the education establishment is misdirected and misinformed. Parents and potential employers have some legitimate complaints, and effort must be expended trying to address those complaints.

Much of the problem can be laid at the feet of the university system. It turns out an overwhelming number of the K-12 teachers. Our schools of education need to be reformed in the ways suggested above under the direction of the greater university. In a larger sense, the 220,000 students who attend the university must be prepared for a modern world where they can communicate in speech, writing and technologically. They must be taught to think, be problem solvers, to be innovators, who can work well in groups. This does not mean turning our universities into tech schools, but we must prepare them to participate in the modern workplace.

VOTER TURNOUT

In 2014 and 2016 voter turnout will be crucial. In 2008 Obama won because so many minorities and young voters went to the polls. Those voters generally do not turn out in large numbers in mid-term elections. As a recent piece in the *New York Times* noted, "The state is divided between older, more culturally southern and conservative voters and younger, more diverse and more liberal voters." The gap between those two groups is "among the most pronounced in the country." Romney won the senior vote by 29 points, while in 2008 Obama won the younger voters by a 35-point margin. The author goes on to note that it is much harder to get the younger voters out for the midterms. "When the young voters stay home, the state reverts to its Republican past and the more conservative bent of the South." (*New York Times* "Midterm Calculus" 28 April, 2014). This problem has been evident for a long time. Remember the Graham/Smith election when 42,000 voters who had supported Dr. Frank the first time, failed to show up the second time.

Add to this the efforts by the Republicans to discourage young voters and the Democrats have a real problem. The only solution is a coordinated, well-funded ground game in 2014, which could have an echo effect on 2016. In 2010 the White House ran its own campaign in North Carolina, separate and distinct from the local races. This can't happen again. Everyone must work together to turn out all voters, Democratic as well as independent and unaffiliated. And although it pains me to say so, this effort must be overseen by some organizations more effective than the state Democratic Party. Only by encouraging and focusing public outrage at what the Tea Party Republicans have done to the state can more progressive candidates be elected.

NORTH CAROLINA JUDICIARY

While the politicized supreme court will continue to be a problem, something can and must be done about the judiciary in North Carolina. As already noted, millions of out-of-state dollars flooded into the state in 2012 to defeat Sam Ervin, who was running for the state Supreme Court. In the 2014 primary, $1,125,000 was spent by outside groups, $650,000 was from the RSLC, to defeat Justice Robin Hudson, a highly qualified and non-ideological candidate for reelection. The only way to stop this attempt to impose a conservative, ideological court system is to eliminate the practice of running for judicial office. Over time North Carolina had gone for non-partisan elections for judges below the Supreme Court and a public financing by way of the Judicial Campaign Reform Act of 2002. For some reason the Republicans didn't like the public funding of the election of judges, or anyone else for that matter, so in their 2013 session they wrapped together in their voter repression efforts photo IDs; shortened early voting; allowing more money in elections; and repealing the state's public financing laws, including those applied to the judicial system (see www.publiccampaign.org). This was definitely a step backward and must be overturned.

But what really must be overturned is the entire practice of electing members of the judiciary. This is particularly urgent in the face of Citizens United. Twenty-four states already use bipartisan commissions to help choose Supreme Court justices. Keeping in mind Lewis Powell's comments about the power of the judiciary, only by getting rid of elections, which are in fact partisan, can we insure an impartial justice system.

$$$ IN POLITICS

The root cause of many of our problems is money in politics. While we should be aware of the problems inherent in enacting campaign finance reform, it should not deter us from hacking away at our pernicious system. Things are only going to get worse as we approach the general election. Already in North Carolina we have seen $18 million pour into the state to undermine Kay Hagan even before she had an opponent. At the very least, they should pass legislation requiring that the donors behind PACS and 501(c) 3s & 4s be revealed. Currently donors can remain anonymous until after elections, a practice the court has not ruled on.

Interestingly enough, in the 2014 Republican Primary, out-of-state money swamped the state. Walter Jones in the 3rd Congressional District successfully defended his seat, despite $1.4 million spent to oust him. "That is not America," said Jones. "That's not democracy. It's the people's government. Not the millionaires' government."

What do I find so amusing or ironic about this? In 2010 and 2012 most Republicans were delighted to see dark money used against Democrats. Republicans professed to love the Citizens United decision (which brought the dark money into campaigns) – unless they find themselves the target of out-of-state millions. As the old saying goes, what goes around comes around. Maybe if this happens often enough, we will get a bi-partisan effort to the money that buys speech out of politics.

PROGRESS BOARD

Next there is a need for a new Progress Board to set goals and measure success in reaching those goals. It is all well and good to make journalistic comments about which state North Carolina compares itself to, but what are the facts? If the traditionalists are so confident that they are going to "fix" North Carolina, then they ought to be eager to submit their results to analysis. How are we doing in the eight old categories the Progress Board tracked, or maybe we should set up new benchmarks. Is the per capita income of our citizens going up? Is our environment as clean as it should be? Is government as transparent as we would like? Is our healthcare sufficient to the need? Are more or fewer people living in poverty? These are all basic measures of the state's well being and we should have some objective way of measuring them. If not a Progress Board, then let's have a state agency staffed with independent professionals protected, at a minimum, by the State Personnel Act so they can provide unbiased data. With this information in hand, voters could make informed decisions about how their elected officials are doing and officials could have a list of things that need to be done. The fact that Governor McCrory, then current chairman of the Southern Growth Policies Board, decided to close down that group which issued regular reports on the South and its progress is yet another sign that metrics regarding development aren't wanted.

There are those who feel that a private, non-partisan entity would be a good alternative to the Progress Board. A new private, not-for-profit successor to the North Carolina Progress Board, with diverse, representative leadership, would give us an invaluable tool for monitoring the state's performance ensuring its accountability and promoting our competitiveness. Civic Way is such an entity.

THE JOHN LOCKE FOUNDATION

Finally, there needs to be formed an organization to counter the John Locke Foundation. Forward thinkers like the late William Friday long advanced the idea that a progressive or modernizing group was needed to balance the influence of the traditionalist or libertarian Locke organization. Ten years ago it was hoped that Z. Smith Reynolds or some group of wealthy individuals would fund such an effort, but there was neither the urgency nor the funds needed to get it off the ground. Now there is the urgency, but the funding is still in question. There have been organizations started, like Progress North Carolina, but they don't yet have the status or the cohesion needed. Modernizers need to avoid the trap of farming too many competing, however worthy, organizations. Note that there is only one Locke Foundation.

RE-DISTRICTING

As a long-run strategy, the manner of redistricting must be changed. Some other states provide models whereby using an independent commission leads to a more balanced outcome. Voters choosing their representatives rather than representatives choosing their voters is the concept. Polls consistently show that a bi-partisan group of North Carolinians supports changing the way election maps are drawn (see North Carolinians for Redistricting Reform website). Recently Richard Vinroot, former Republican Mayor of Charlotte and Charles Meeker, former Democratic Mayor of Raleigh, have been trying to rally support to end partisan gerrymandering. Even influential Republican legislators like Paul Stam (Wake) have supported giving the job or redistricting to a non-partisan legislative staff committee when it comes time to redistrict in 2021; and even Art Pope sees the logic of a commission. Whether that support will hold firm remains to be seen, but note that we are talking about 2021, by which time many things will have changed, including the entire direction of the state.

THE DEMOCRATIC PARTY

No one will deny that the North Carolina State Democratic Party is in disarray. The previous party chair was David Parker, who has to take some of the blame for the losses in 2012. Under attack by party members who were still smarting from the "shellacking" in 2010, Parker never could gain traction. Raising money without a legislative majority and without war horses like Marc Basnight and Tony Rand was very difficult, but it generally is harder for the party out of power to raise money. When the election for a new chair was held, it turned into a knock-down, drag-out fight. When the dust cleared, Randy Voller, the mayor of Pittsboro (population 3,743) had defeated former Congressman Bob Ethridge by 11 votes (It was not hard to compare Voller to Sarah Palin, the former mayor of Wasilla, Alaska, population 7,831). Voller was immediately embroiled in controversy over unpaid personal taxes. But there were other complaints. As Bob Geary states in an article in the *Independent*, the "rap" on Voller is that he is "arrogant, divisive, lacks rudimentary political judgment or interpersonal skills and is oblivious to the need to avoid even the appearance of improper conduct." As Gary Pearce, Jim Hunt's former press secretary, put it, Voller should resign and "go back to work and pay off (his) taxes." Many within the party think that Voller's greatest sin is "thinking he should have run for chairman in the first place."

Despite the criticism, Voller has held on, and at the most recent party convention, despite a threatened effort to remove him as chairman, a sullen crowd resolved to avoid further infighting and let him stay. Meanwhile the Republicans elected Art Pope's cousin, Claude Pope, as their Party chairman.

The Democratic meeting illustrated the problems facing the feckless state party. Some wanted to throw Voller out and start anew; others wanted to try and paper over the split in order to begin preparing for local elections and 2014. Others thought that there had to be a reform effort starting within the local party organizations since the party tended to resist top-down management. It all reminded one of the old aphorisms: "Are you a member of an organized political party? No, I'm a Democrat." But let's face it, something has to be done.

One of the things we should have learned from the past is that the individual and their inability to attract acolytes is more important than party. This was true of Simmons, Gardner, Hunt and Helms. They dominated the party, not vice versa.

Given the party's tradition, it is hard to imagine a coup to unseat Voller. A better solution would be to mount an organized effort, including paid staff, to work to reorganize the party from the ground up. The problem is leadership for any such reform effort. Someone or a group of someones needs to step forward if the party is to mount a grass roots reformation.

Another option is to simply ignore the party and set up an independent organization to raise money and endorse particular candidates. If the Hunt model were to be followed it would mean finding a skilled, charismatic individual with the vision to establish an independent organization. There is good reason to support such an effort. For one thing it would focus on what is really important – electing people who have a modernist agenda regardless of their affiliation, if any. It also might be more likely to attract a very important voting bloc – the independent or unaffiliated voter. If this were to be the course selected there should be an understanding right up front that it is going to take a lot of money to defeat the Republicans and their deep-pocketed friends. Leadership and money would have to be directed toward the new organization and not the party.

If a new party were to be formed, careful thought needs to be given to its platform. Some conservatives have suggested that the Democratic Party began to lose voters when it gave priority to a whole range of social issues. If this is correct, a new party should narrow its focus and give priority to economic issues. The old "jobs, jobs, jobs" mantra that worked so well for the Republicans does have a certain resonance. There is no end to the list of economic issues that can be attached to the jobs program. Unemployment remains high and new techniques need to be found to bring it down. While environmentalism has lost some of its allure, conservationism has not. The point here simply being that themes that unify voters should be highlighted and other issues, while still on the agenda, given a less prominent role. Income inequality is growing and threatens the middle class. Regulations on the financial industry are woefully lax, thus threatening another Great Recession.

Whichever course is taken, a lot of thought needs to go into the platform or list of issues upon which to focus. This is always difficult for modernizer movements, which tend to be a coalition of minorities. But it is here that the discipline comes in; the more disparate the issues chosen, the more targets you offer the opposition. Therefore, there would be wisdom in focusing on issues that have historically resonated in North Carolina. There is a clear connection here with the economy, and building support within the business community is essential for educational improvement. This won't be as easy as it once was; yet it is a top priority. Historically the business community has called the shots; they must be convinced that the current course is disastrous for them and that a more modernist alternative holds promise. Obviously people like Jim Goodnight and Brad Wilson see the connection – the recognition must become more widespread. We must also recognize that North Carolina needs an array of businesses, some low-wage, some knowledge-based and some new and innovative. Most particularly, North Carolina needs businesses that do not detract from the quality of life.

A basic issue must be education, and by education it must be clear that this means K-16 and beyond. A seamless and comprehensive educational opportunity for North Carolina's students must come at the top of any agenda. There is no longer any question that a focus of the current Redeemer legislators is to undermine public education. By way of private school vouchers, low teacher pay (46th in the country) and other disincentives, they have set about dismantling an already shaky public school structure. Public education has always been a target for Art Pope, a graduate of UNC Chapel Hill.

The third element would be voter inclusiveness. Anyone with any sense of democratic values understands that in a democracy, you want as many people to vote as possible. North Carolina has had a checkered history in this regard. Prior to 1835 there was a property-holding qualification for voting and, of course, even after 1835 black people couldn't vote. In 1865 North Carolina was forced, via the 14th and 15th Amendments, to allow voting by all male citizens. This right was essentially taken away by the new North Carolina Constitution of 1898, which found ways to block blacks from voting. Only in 1965 did blacks regain the right of suffrage. And, of course, women couldn't vote until 1920, and it wasn't until 1971 that North Carolina ratified the 19th Amendment, thereby formally allowing them the right to suffrage. In the 1980s Jesse successfully led the fight against the Equal Rights Amendment preventing gender discrimination.

Finally, whatever the organizational solution chosen, the modernizers need to begin *now* to select candidates. Finding some new, fresh faces should be a priority, and some emphasis needs to be put on youth and diversity. The previous leadership is aging out and any successful effort in the future must include more women and minorities. Of course, the experienced leaders like Jim Hunt, Bob Ethridge, Tony Rand, David Price, Mel Watt, Beverly Perdue, Kay Hagan, and others need to be involved, but if one is looking to 2016 and beyond, there needs to be a new crop. A good place to start might be in the alumni of the Morehead Scholars program at Chapel Hill and the Park Scholars at N. C. State. Both organizations strive to select and develop leaders. There also are the scores of political aspirants trained by the Institute of Political Leadership (IOPL).

IN SUMMARY

The progress we made in the 20th Century is not the whole story; too often we've made advances only to slide back into our less admirable past.

There have been multiple efforts to move the state forward: the Murphy plan in 1815, the Whig initiative in the 1830s, the Reconstruction effort in the late 1860s; the Fusionists in 1894 and finally, the high-water mark of the modernist movement in the sixty years after 1950. In each case, the forward movement has been followed by a retrograde one, and that retrograde movement had set back North Carolina educationally and economically. Even by the beginning of 21st century, we were not where we would have wanted to be and surely did not have so secure a position that we could experiment with old ideas that have failed.

A recurring factor in North Carolina political history is the power of the business class, sometimes predominantly traditionalist, sometimes modernist. Several different groups of oligarchs have wielded power. Originally it was the big plantation owners who made up the landed gentry; although relatively few in number, they had disproportionate influence. They were the slave owners who helped lead the state into the Civil War. Then came the leaders of the textile, furniture and tobacco industry. Finally, there were the bankers, financiers, real estate magnates and technology innovators. At least for the past fifty years, this later group of business people has generally supported education, internal improvements and an environment that will contribute to quality of life and attract more investment. If any new party is to win over the state, they must have the business support.

There has always been present in the state a deeply ingrained southern traditionalist strain. For much of 200 years (1815 – 2010), that traditionalism could be translated as racism. But there were other strains as well, including classism, xenophobia, and misogyny. Even when championing forward movement, modernist leaders always need to be careful not to get too far out in front, lest they offer too tempting a target.

The party that has been the modernizing one has changed through two centuries. In the 1830s through 1850s, Whigs were the progressive party. After the Civil War, the Republicans, who were modernizers, ran the state only from 1865 to 1871. Some former Whigs joined the Republicans, but were known by the Democratic opposition as "Scalawags." The Democratic Party held control in North Carolina from 1871 to 1894 and then from 1898 through 2010. They began as traditionalists and then became the modernizers. Still, as mid-20th century modernizers, many Democrats opposed civil rights and some could be called racists. This provided the pivotal point. President Richard Nixon saw in the Civil Rights Act of 1964 and Voting Rights Act of 1965 an opportunity to pry the South out of the Democratic column. Relying on the lingering white supremacist sentiment in the South, the Republican Party positioned itself to the right of the Democrats. The Republicans became the traditionalists, leaving the modernizers to the Democrats. The traditionalist forces opposing change were never lacking powerful leaders from Zebulon Vance to Jesse Helms. But it was Helms who mounted the most sustained opposition, starting in 1960 and carrying the banner until his death in 2008. It was in that year that North Carolina surprised the nation by voting for Barack Obama. But two years later, the current movement to the right began in earnest, with the Republican sweep of the General Assembly.

The conventional wisdom is that over the last twenty years the Republican Party took over the solidly Democratic South, but a case can be made that the South took over the Republican Party. This is particularly true in regard to the race issue. Whereas Nixon and many mainstream Republicans were to the right of many mainstream Democrats regarding race issues, they were not nearly as intransigent on the race issue as many southerners were. Governor George Wallace of Alabama, Governor Lester Maddox of Georgia, and Senator Theodore Bilbo of Mississippi were unabashed white supremacists and they reflected the views of many of their constituents. So, when the Republicans brought the South under their tent, they knowingly, but more likely unknowingly, brought virulent racism as well.

Starting with Ronald Reagan, limiting government became a mantra for the Republican Party. It was Reagan who made a connection between welfare and government ineptitude. He also opposed the Civil Rights Act of 1964 and the Voting Rights Act of 1965, basing his opposition on constitutional and states' rights grounds. It was easy, however, for those southerners whose opposition was more nearly on grounds of race to see Reagan as a champion for their cause. It also was easy to begin to link welfare with minorities and minorities with government. Thus antigovernment rhetoric took on a whiff of racism. To oppose "government" became opposition to programs that supposedly coddled and rewarded lazy minorities who were feeding at the public trough.

However, many Republicans never totally bought into the traditionalists' mantra. Though these Republicans were suspicious of big government, unenthusiastic about many regulations, and generally opposed to higher taxes, they were supportive of public education and a modern infrastructure. Moreover, they were distinctly not racists. Governors Holshouser and Martin were both representative of this group, as were many business people.

It is my contention that the current group of Republicans is a break with the Holshouser/Martin model. If they resemble anything historically, they would be Democrats from the 1898 period. Yet even that does not capture their unique nature. They combine something of the old Democrats with a generous mixture of Libertarianism. At present what they want to build is not as clear as what they want to tear down.

Like many others, I was shocked at the radical rightward turn of the Republican/Tea Partiers in 2010 to 2013. Conventional wisdom was that they would have moved cautiously in order to avoid overreaching, thereby alienating middle-of-the-road voters. Instead, their moves were sweeping in their range and ideological extremism. Teachers, government workers, taxes, regulations, social issues, women, voting rights, were all attacked with equal abandon. How could they be so reckless? There are several possible explanations. One is that they didn't expect to be in power long and wanted to get as much done during their short tenure as possible. Another, and a more likely explanation, is that they felt secure behind the dual firewalls of redistricting and voter repression. These moves, they hoped, would make them bulletproof. And they may well be right. If they can hold unchallenged power, the House, the Senate and the governorship until 2021, they will be able to set the state back a century. I am increasingly convinced that they want to trash the Grand Bargain, repeal the New Deal, the Progressive Era and go back to the 1890s. Coincidentally, Karl Rove says that his model President was William McKinley, 1897 – 1901. Moreover, the start of Federal regulation of business was the Sherman Anti Trust Act of 1890 and the hated Income Tax came under Woodrow Wilson in 1913. Oh, it was so much better before these Federal intrusions!

The only way to stop them is to start taking the state back now. The defeat of Kay Hagan would be yet another victory for the Koch brothers. The election of 2016 provides an opportunity to replace McCrory with Roy Cooper or some other yet-to-emerge candidate as well as to further erode legislative majorities. Those who long to return to a modernist N. C. must realize that each election counts, not just presidential ones. The road back won't be easy, and it will be breathtaking only in regards to the breath needed for a long upward slog. We are fighting a national battle against the retrograde forces and the out-of-state millions that would take the whole country backward. Since they seem to want to turn the clock back, maybe we should take inspiration from Teddy Roosevelt's rallying cry against the plutocrats at the Progressive Party Convention in 1913 when he said, "We stand at Armageddon and we battle for the Lord."

Literary imagination is replete with stories of time travel. We have Mark Twain's *A Connecticut Yankee in King Arthur's Court*; we have the movie, *Back to the Future*, wherein a wacky scientist moves backward and forward through time. But seldom in real life do we have cases where nostalgia for an imaginary better, simpler past has driven a state or a nation's political course. Can you imagine a Germany wanting to return to the 1940s or a Russia wanting to revisit the excesses of Joseph Stalin? Or, how about deciding to substitute a 19th century transportation system for a 21st century one? But this is tantamount to what is happening in North Carolina today. Rejecting science, fearing complexity, dismissing new ideas, closing their eyes to our demographic future, our current leaders want to turn back the clock.

North Carolina and her people stand at a crossroads – we have been here before. We can either go forward, we can stand still, or we can go backward. In the past, in different eras, we have tried each of these strategies. We know that going forward takes effort and we have never gotten to be as good a state as we would like. We also know what going backward nets us; we are about to find out again unless we reverse course and fast. Voter suppression, low taxes, lax regulation, and poor public schools won't even get us halfway home.

Have we lost all ambition? Have we lost our competitive edge? Are we satisfied to be mediocre? Don't we want a better life for those who follow us? Do we want clear air, clean water, tree-capped mountains, and pristine beaches? Or, will we surrender to those negative forces that had been in retreat for fifty years? And don't kid yourselves, those malignant forces, driven by ignorance, intolerance, and mean-spiritedness are now setting a lot of North Carolina's agenda.

I am convinced that the majority of North Carolina's people, regardless of political affiliation, and even those with no political affiliation, don't want to go back to the Gilded Age of white supremacy and inequality. And if you think my reference to white supremacy is an exaggeration, look at those in majority in the North Carolina General Assembly. There is not a black or brown face among them, although black and brown citizens make up fully one third of our population. Would those policies on Medicaid, unemployment insurance, the Earned Income Tax Credit, and public schools be passed by a more representative legislature? I don't think so.

So, this is a call to arms for all those good people, regardless of race or party or age or status, to come to the defense of the Old North State. This is an appeal to our better angels. The rest of the world and most states are moving on, trying new ideas, daring to dream, opening their borders and their minds to new citizens; unless we revise course soon, we will be swept aside by those more progressive states. Our schools will stagnate, our roads and bridges will crumble, our environment will sour. That is not for me and I hope not for you. Together we can reverse course, stake out a better tomorrow, grasp time by the forelock and move boldly into the future. Our past tells us that we have overcome the forces of negativity before – surely we will again.

NORTH CAROLINA PROGRESS BOARD REPORT
SUMMARY

PREFACE

North Carolina is undergoing rapid change – in its population, economy and natural resources. Of all the predictions for the future, only one seems certain. More change will come, and it will come with ever-increasing speed. As North Carolinians, our challenge is to ensure that these changes 1) bring health and prosperity for all citizens and 2) preserve and enhance the state's environment and quality of life. The North Carolina Progress Board was created to help answer this challenge.

As part of its mission to set strategic targets for the state, and track our progress in achieving those targets, the North Carolina Progress Board presents the 2005 North Carolina 20/20 Update Report. This report is intended to discharge one of the Progress Board's statutory duties – to report biennially on key performance trends and provide information about strategic issues that are likely to shape our state's future qualify of life. We believe that the contents of this report, which can be found in more detail (www.ncprogress.org) will interest everyone who is committed to making North Carolina the best state in the Southeast and, ultimately, the nation.

The North Carolina Progress Board served as an independent proponent for strategic action and accountability. Specifically, the mission is to keep leaders and citizens alike focused on the big picture: the long-term goals and needs of our state and its people. This means serving as a strategic compass – identifying critical issues, setting milestones, checking progress, reporting data, recommending course corrections, and reporting imaginative solutions to jumpstart change.

The General Assembly established the North Carolina Progress Board as a permanent entity of state government in 1995. Its 24 members are appointed by the governor, the leadership of the N.C. House and Senate, and the board itself. Over the next six years, the Progress Board worked with citizens, public officials and many others to elaborate on the vision first drafted by the Commission for a Competitive North Carolina. The effort culminated in 2001 with the *North Carolina 20/20 Report*, a comprehensive report describing the challenges facing the state and presenting goals and targets for improvement in all eight issue areas.

Throughout this process and even after the release of the *North Carolina 20/20 Report*, the Progress Board sought to involve citizens in debating the state's priorities for the future. We met with community groups and spoke with legislative groups, local leaders and advocacy organizations. Our work showed us the deep commitment North Carolinians have for our state and the deep perplexity many feel about the state budget. In answer, the Progress Board in 2003 released *Our State, Our Money — A citizens/ Guide to the North Carolina Budget*, a guide explaining how budget decisions are made, sources and uses of money and how citizens can affect the process.

The report was broken into eight imperatives and then further subdivided into targets intended to reach these goals. The imperatives were: 1) Healthy Children and Families; 2) Safe and Vibrant Communities; 3) Quality Education For All; 4) A High Performance Workforce; 5) A Sustainable Environment; 6) A Prosperous Economy; 7) A 21st Century Infrastructure and 8) Active Citizenship and Accountable Government.

From Robert E. Tyndall, former dean of a school of education and national consultant on education matters:

> Clearly, the potential for collaboration across the political aisles is diminished and nowhere is the erosion of trust and support more pronounced than when it comes to our public schools. The prevailing public perception that schools are at the center of societal change has achieved widespread acceptance. While some still hold firm to the belief that our schools are the foundation of social and economic mobility others see

them as broken and dysfunctional. Critics of public education frequently cite declining academic performance and a host of general indicators of decline such as drug use, teen pregnancy and violence as powerful support of their assertions that today's schools are failing our society. Ironically, many of these same critics lament the declining support for societal bedrock institutions such as the family, religion and church while simultaneously arguing for the abandonment of an affordable, high quality public education for all. It would be dishonest not to acknowledge that much of the reversal in support for public education is driven by the belief by some that schools have been co-opted by a progressive ideology rooted as much in a social and political agenda as in education, self-reliance or economic mobility. Those who attempt to acknowledge the validity of poor school performance data, while at the same time attempting to broaden the cause-and- effect relationship and portray schools as suspended in a complex web of social, economic, political and shifting cultural norms are often accused of intentionally confounding the facts. Few subjects ignite passion as dose the issue of school support.

It was inevitable that those concerned about the inadequacy of schools would eventually expand their criticism to the institutions of higher education where educators are prepared. They assert that if schools are failing, then teachers must be a major part of the problem and question, "Who prepares teachers?" It is becoming increasingly apparent that old arguments put forth by schools of education about being once or twice removed from the student-teacher interactions in schools will no longer buy universities immunity from such criticisms. However complex the reality may be, the perceived relationship is established as a simple and powerful equation. Colleges and universities, which for the most part stood by as interested and sympathetic but distant observers when public schools were being attacked, now find themselves at the center of the debate. Legislators and their diverse publics seek to find ways to fit the accountability harness to university faculty.

Educator preparation programs that seek to be viewed as part of the solution must accept the perception that they also can be part of the problem. They cannot continue to respond to such complex problems in generalities and disengage themselves from a concerned public. Today's climate requires proactive participation in improving schools by being honest about limitations and clear about what colleges and universities can and cannot do. Just as public schools once attempted to be all things to all people, partially in response to cumulative external mandates, colleges and universities must be cautious not to fall into the same trap. Colleges and universities must tell their stories clearly and frequently if the public is to understand that they must assist in- but cannot drive-school reform. True systemic reform will require a candid and aggressive partnership with public schools and the general public. All must understand their roles and accept joint credit for successes and responsibility for failures. Those of us who have watched this shift in trust and support play out understand that all citizens have a right to be in this discussion and that punishing schools and schools of education for being tone deaf in the past will undermine the quality of life for all of us in the future. This conversation will require leadership with a capital "L" to find common ground before decades of progress are reversed.

At the core of any effort to rebuild public trust is the requirement that universities acknowledge that their most important work occurs not on campus, but in the classrooms where their graduates practice their craft. They must engage the student experience and see their work as faculty through the lens of the students of their students. This view does not diminish the work of researchers and theorists, but it does call into question the importance of such work when it is not embedded in practice and openly judged on the basis of the ultimate test crucible, the school classroom. Without this vital linkage the work of university faculty will be viewed as increasingly irrelevant. When we look into our students' eyes, we must see the eyes of their students. Schools of education must start this honest dialogue by inviting courageous conversations about roles, relationships and responsibilities and acknowledging that public schools and the public have as much right and responsibility as they to engage in conversations about transforming schools of education to make them more relevant, meaningful and accountable.

As the debate on whether a college degree is framed as a public or a private trust continues, successful and engaged schools of education recognize the need to participate actively in the creation and support of partnerships designed to assist public schools. Such programs can help schools improve through field-based assistance and research and through redesigned, relevant and responsible educator preparation programs. Responsible programs must share accountability for the performance of the public school students. Some programs have acknowledged this linkage and shared responsibility, but the vast majority continue to offer topical courses that often reflect popular movements of the day rather than balancing their curriculums with validated, best practices in reading, math, science or historical analysis that will matter in the school classroom and life. This realization calls for strong partnerships with schools vested in "knowledge work" and performance results. Colleges and universities are not being asked to abandon thoughtful and balanced discussion about social justice, gender rights or diversity; they must, however, ensure that these discussions do not overwhelm the need for the hard work of being competent professionals who can master the classroom and engage, challenge and graduate students who have a solid academic base, curious minds, and the ability to apply knowledge to improve their lives and their communities. Both results are important and possible.

The sheer magnitude of reversing negative public perception without losing the driving force of an effective and respected public education system is deeply rooted in the historical backdrop of each region. The prevalence of low incomes, limited employment opportunities, meager educational aspirations and insufficient local resources are significant factors shaping the narrative throughout North Carolina. These complex historical antecedents account for much of the current frustration, yet our state's colleges and universities have much that is good to tell and little time to get the word out before waning public confidence turns to outright abandonment. North Carolina cannot reverse decades of commitment to education just as the global knowledge ecology explodes around them.

To counter the perceptions that little, if anything, is being done to improve public schools and teacher preparation, schools of education must offer evidence that they are listening and are ahead of the curve when it comes to recognizing the symbiotic relationship that should exist among colleges/universities, public schools and the health of our communities. Examples from leaders in this effort include, but are not limited to, the following:

• Uniformly rigorous admission requirements that include screening applicants on the basis of academic performance including baseline GPA requirements in basic studies, success on a battery of national exams focusing on general knowledge and specialty area content knowledge normed in the top performance quartile, and specified exit examinations/demonstrations focusing on content, pedagogy and technology.

• Real double major requirements, which ensure discipline-specific content mastery along with methodology and pedagogical preparation to dispel the "academic weak sister" image of schools of education.

• Establishing a campus Office of Service to Public Schools focusing the resources of the entire campus on school assistance as well as developing a special plan to support designated low-performing districts. This includes aggressive and creative recruitment and financial support for low income and underrepresented populations.

• Creating regional education consortia designed to combine the talents, energy and resources of public schools, community colleges, businesses and the university. Such collaboration has led to a number of nationally -recognized school improvement initiatives. Many of the consortia begun in prior decades failed to focus on important work, did not negotiate true partner relations that encouraged mutual assessment, joint funding, leveraged purchasing power or joint appointments. These solutions are needed now more than ever. These partnerships require high levels of commitment and even some of the most successful models faded as leadership changed or objectives became less focused.

• Produce both Faculty assistance directories and reciprocal public school faculty assistance directories that outline individual expertise and describe how to access support and actively make the connections happen. Public schools can provide invaluable expertise to universities and can help create integrated work models. Both entities have much to offer, but in most cases the colleges and universities host events and create academic programs in insular environments rather than creating functional work teams. Together we need to heed Phil Schletchty's advice and get busy "working on the work that matters."

• Create comprehensive technology initiatives to ensure that all graduates of educator preparation programs have mastered "essential technology skills" and can demonstrate such mastery. Further, Regional Educational Consortia can assist practicing educators in public schools by offering a host of technology outreach initiatives.

The verdict is still out on how online instruction will impact learning and institutional relationships and identity. Will this digital engagement create deep and continuing support for education or will cheaper, better, faster result in increased access but decreased public support or alumni loyalty? There is much work to be done to link online instruction for teachers and administrators to results in real school classrooms.

• Establish Science and Math Education Centers, located on campuses and in public schools. These models have shown significant results when designed in close partnership with schools. Results include summer venture programs that provide advanced institutes for interested and academically able high school students, teacher renewal programs, and classroom-based research projects. .

• Strengthen articulation agreements designed to provide seamless access to educational opportunities and to allow movement from high school to community colleges to universities. These agreements along with new off-campus degree programs and weekend colleges are examples of innovative ways schools of education can join hands in their regions to benefit from collaboration and educational cooperation.

• Maintain a visible presence in schools and school districts. Model Clinical Teaching Programs and Professional Development Systems that take their programs to schools require faculty engagement in the field and are managed jointly, are potentially powerful models for public schools and schools of education. When educators understand that these models are not about workshops- often called "professional development", but are about developing and strengthening the profession, then powerful partnerships can emerge. Ironically, during these difficult budget times many schools of education are withdrawing to the campus when their presence and these partnerships are needed most. The best models ensure an integrated educator preparation approach involving universities and public schools in all aspects of design and delivery including teacher preparation, recruitment, induction, evaluation and continuous learning. Such models remove the walls that often separate universities and public schools, create new roles and relationships for teachers and college/university faculty, and guarantee intensive developmental supervision for student interns. Institutions that are justifying using technology alone to mentor future teachers in the field using videos and web observations alone fail to understand the full significance and power of a site presence. When university faculty work in schools they are sending a powerful message about the importance of the work being done there, are experiencing the world of education through the student lens, making a visible statement to their interns and are establishing social relationships that will open doors for future collaboration.

Given the failure of some institutions to develop deep partnerships and the abandonment of collaborative initiatives by others, it is not surprising that many critics of higher education are increasing the volume of their criticism. Clearly, schools of education must engage in conversations characterized by mutual regard, redouble their efforts to have a strong and visible presence in their regions to improve schools and to ensure that it is clear that they have skin in the game. Through such efforts colleges and universities can assist public schools in creating conditions that foster and sustain new levels of competence in schools and on campuses.

When schools of education immerse themselves in the work of schools and initiate efforts like some of those described above, then important results can be realized. These initiatives are pieces of the puzzle of school improvement. With a broader understanding of the unique roles of colleges and universities in the overall effort and increased understanding of the complexities of the problems, we can recover the central place of education in North Carolina's future. Schools of education need to talk less, listen more, and live and breathe linking their work to student learning in schools and engage every citizen in this critical conversation.

CONFIDENTIAL MEMORANDUM

Attack on American Free Enterprise System

DATE: August 23, 1971

TO: Mr. Eugene B. Sydnor, Jr., Chairman, Education Committee, U.S. Chamber of Commerce

FROM: Lewis F. Powell, Jr.

This memorandum is submitted at your request as a basis for the discussion on August 24 with Mr. Booth (executive vice president) and others at the U.S. Chamber of Commerce. The purpose is to identify the problem, and suggest possible avenues of action for further consideration.

Dimensions of the Attack

No thoughtful person can question that the American economic system is under broad attack. This varies in scope, intensity, in the techniques employed, and in the level of visibility.

There always have been some who opposed the American system, and preferred socialism or some form of statism (communism or fascism). Also, there always have been critics of the system, whose criticism has been wholesome and constructive so long as the objective was to improve rather than to subvert or destroy.

But what now concerns us is quite new in the history of America. We are not dealing with sporadic or isolated attacks from a relatively few extremists or even from the minority socialist cadre. Rather, the assault on the enterprise system is broadly based and consistently pursued. It is gaining momentum and converts.

Sources of the Attack

The sources are varied and diffused. They include, not unexpectedly, the Communists, New Leftists and other revolutionaries who would destroy the entire system, both political and economic. These extremists of the left are far more numerous, better financed, and increasingly are more welcomed and encouraged by other elements of society, than ever before in our history. But they remain a small minority, and are not yet the principal cause for concern.

The most disquieting voices joining the chorus of criticism come from perfectly respectable elements of society: from the college campus, the pulpit, the media, the intellectual and literary journals, the arts and sciences, and from politicians. In most of these groups the movement against the system is participated in only by minorities. Yet, these often are the most articulate, the most vocal, the most prolific in their writing and speaking.

Moreover, much of the media — for varying motives and in varying degrees — either voluntarily accords unique publicity to these "attackers," or at least allows them to exploit the media for their purposes. This is especially true of television, which now plays such a predominant role in shaping the thinking, attitudes and emotions of our people. One of the bewildering paradoxes of our time is the extent to which the enterprise system tolerates, if not participates in, its own destruction.

The campuses from which much of the criticism emanates are supported by (i) tax funds generated largely from American business, and (ii) contributions from capital funds controlled or generated by American business. The boards of trustees of our universities overwhelmingly are composed of men and women who are leaders in the system.

Most of the media, including the national TV systems, are owned and theoretically controlled by corporations which depend upon profits, and the enterprise system to survive.

Tone of the Attack

This memorandum is not the place to document in detail the tone, character, or intensity of the attack. The following quotations will suffice to give one a general idea:

William Kunstler, warmly welcomed on campuses and listed in a recent student poll as the "American lawyer most admired," incites audiences as follows:

"You must learn to fight in the streets, to revolt, to shoot guns. We will learn to do all of the things that property owners fear." The New Leftists who heed Kunstler's advice increasingly are beginning to act — not just against military recruiting offices and manufacturers of munitions, but against a variety of businesses: "Since February, 1970, branches (of Bank of America) have been attacked 39 times, 22 times with explosive devices and 17 times with fire bombs or by arsonists." Although New Leftist spokesmen are succeeding in radicalizing thousands of the young, the greater cause for concern is the hostility of respectable liberals and social reformers. It is the sum total of their views and influence which could indeed fatally weaken or destroy the system."

A chilling description of what is being taught on many of our campuses was written by Stewart Alsop:

"Yale, like every other major college, is graduating scores of bright young men who are practitioners of 'the politics of despair.' These young men despise the American political and economic system . . . (their) minds seem to be wholly closed. They live, not by rational discussion, but by mindless slogans." A recent poll of students on 12 representative campuses reported that: "Almost half the students favored socialization of basic U.S. industries."

A visiting professor from England at Rockford College gave a series of lectures entitled "The Ideological War Against Western Society," in which he documents the extent to which members of the intellectual community are waging ideological warfare against the enterprise system and the values of western society. In a foreword to these lectures, famed Dr. Milton Friedman of Chicago warned: "It (is) crystal clear that the foundations of our free society are under wide-ranging and powerful attack — not by Communist or any other conspiracy but by misguided individuals parroting one another and unwittingly serving ends they would never intentionally promote."

Perhaps the single most effective antagonist of American business is

Ralph Nader, who — thanks largely to the media — has become a legend in his own time and an idol of millions of Americans. A recent article in Fortune speaks of Nader as follows:

> "The passion that rules in him — and he is a passionate man — is aimed at smashing utterly the target of his hatred, which is corporate power. He thinks, and says quite bluntly, that a great many corporate executives belong in prison — for defrauding the consumer with shoddy merchandise, poisoning the food supply with chemical additives, and willfully manufacturing unsafe products that will maim or kill the buyer. He emphasizes that he is not talking just about 'fly-by-night hucksters' but the top management of blue chip business."

A frontal assault was made on our government, our system of justice, and the free enterprise system by Yale Professor Charles Reich in his widely publicized book: "The Greening of America," published last winter.

The foregoing references illustrate the broad, shotgun attack on the system itself. There are countless examples of rifle shots which undermine confidence and confuse the public. Favorite current targets are proposals for tax incentives through changes in depreciation rates and investment credits. These are usually described in the media as "tax breaks," "loop holes" or "tax benefits" for the benefit of business. * As viewed by a columnist in the Post, such tax measures would benefit "only the rich, the owners of big companies."

It is dismaying that many politicians make the same argument that tax measures of this kind benefit only "business," without benefit to "the poor." The fact that this is either political demagoguery or economic illiteracy is of slight comfort. This setting of the "rich" against the "poor," of business against the people, is the cheapest and most dangerous kind of politics.

The Apathy and Default of Business

What has been the response of business to this massive assault upon its fundamental economics, upon its philosophy, upon its right to continue to manage its own affairs, and indeed upon its integrity?

The painfully sad truth is that business, including the boards of directors' and the top executives of corporations great and small and business organizations at all levels, often have responded — if at all — by appeasement, ineptitude and ignoring the problem. There are, of course, many exceptions to this sweeping generalization. But the net effect of such response as has been made is scarcely visible.

In all fairness, it must be recognized that businessmen have not been trained or equipped to conduct guerrilla warfare with those who propagandize against the system, seeking insidiously and constantly to sabotage it. The traditional role of business executives has been to manage, to produce, to sell, to create jobs, to make profits, to improve the standard of living, to be community leaders, to serve on charitable and educational boards, and generally to be good citizens. They have performed these tasks very well indeed.

But they have shown little stomach for hard-nose contest with their critics, and little skill in effective intellectual and philosophical debate.

A column recently carried by the *Wall Street Journal* was entitled: "Memo to GM: Why Not Fight Back?" Although addressed to GM by name, the article was a warning to all American business. Columnist St. John said:

> "General Motors, like American business in general, is 'plainly in trouble' because intellectual bromides have been substituted for a sound intellectual exposition of its point of view." Mr. St. John then commented on the tendency of business leaders to compromise with and appease critics. He cited the concessions which Nader wins from management, and spoke of "the fallacious view many businessmen take toward their critics." He drew a parallel to the mistaken tactics of many college administrators: "College administrators learned too late that such appeasement serves to destroy free speech, academic freedom and genuine scholarship. One campus radical demand was conceded by university heads only to be followed by a fresh crop which soon escalated to what amounted to a demand for outright surrender."

One need not agree entirely with Mr. St. John's analysis. But most observers of the American scene will agree that the essence of his message is sound. American business "plainly in trouble"; the response to the wide range of critics has been ineffective, and has included appeasement; the time has come — indeed, it is long overdue — for the wisdom, ingenuity and resources of American business to be marshalled against those who would destroy it.

Responsibility of Business Executives

What specifically should be done? The first essential — a prerequisite to any effective action — is for businessmen to confront this problem as a primary responsibility of corporate management.

The overriding first need is for businessmen to recognize that the ultimate issue may be survival — survival of what we call the free enterprise system, and all that this means for the strength and prosperity of America and the freedom of our people.

The day is long past when the chief executive officer of a major corporation discharges his responsibility by maintaining a satisfactory growth of profits, with due regard to the corporation's public and social responsibilities. If our system is to survive, top management must be equally concerned with protecting and preserving the system itself. This involves far more than an increased emphasis on "public relations" or "governmental affairs" — two areas in which corporations long have invested substantial sums.

A significant first step by individual corporations could well be the designation of an executive vice president (ranking with other executive VP's) whose responsibility is to counter-on the broadest front-the attack on the enterprise system. The public relations department could be one of the foundations assigned to this executive, but his responsibilities should encompass some of the types of activities referred to subsequently in this memorandum. His budget and staff should be adequate to the task.

Possible Role of the Chamber of Commerce

But independent and uncoordinated activity by individual corporations, as important as this is, will not be sufficient. Strength lies in organization, in careful long-range planning and implementation, in consistency of action over an indefinite period of years, in the scale of financing available only through joint effort, and in the political power available only through united action and national organizations.

Moreover, there is the quite understandable reluctance on the part of any one corporation to get too far out in front and to make itself too visible a target.

The role of the National Chamber of Commerce is therefore vital. Other national organizations (especially those of various industrial and commercial groups) should join in the effort, but no other organizations appear to be as well situated as the Chamber. It enjoys a strategic position, with a fine reputation and a broad base of support. Also — and this is of immeasurable merit — there are hundreds of local Chambers of Commerce which can play a vital supportive role.

It hardly need be said that before embarking upon any program, the Chamber should study and analyze possible courses of action and activities, weighing risks against probable effectiveness and feasibility of each. Considerations of cost, the assurance of financial and other support from members, adequacy of staffing and similar problems will all require the most thoughtful consideration.

The Campus

The assault on the enterprise system was not mounted in a few months. It has gradually evolved over the past two decades, barely perceptible in its origins and benefiting (sic) from a gradualism that provoked little awareness much less any real reaction.

Although origins, sources and causes are complex and interrelated, and obviously difficult to identify without careful qualification, there is reason to believe that the campus is the single most dynamic source. The social science faculties usually include members who are unsympathetic to the enterprise system. They may range from a Herbert Marcuse, Marxist faculty member at the University of California at San Diego, and convinced socialists, to the ambivalent liberal critic who finds more to condemn than to commend. Such faculty members need not be in a majority. They are often personally attractive and magnetic; they are stimulating teachers, and their controversy attracts student following; they are prolific writers and lecturers; they author many of the textbooks, and they exert enormous influence — far out of proportion to their numbers — on their colleagues and in the academic world.

Social science faculties (the political scientist, economist, sociologist and many of the historians) tend to be liberally oriented, even when leftists are not present. This is not a criticism per se, as the need for liberal thought is essential to a balanced viewpoint. The difficulty is that "balance" is conspicuous by its absence on many campuses, with relatively few members being of conservatives or moderate persuasion and even the relatively few often being less articulate and aggressive than their crusading colleagues.

This situation extending back many years and with the imbalance gradually worsening, has had an enormous impact on millions of young American students. In an article in Barron's Weekly, seeking an answer to why so many young people are disaffected even to the point of being revolutionaries, it was said: "Because they were taught that way." Or, as noted by columnist Stewart Alsop, writing about his alma mater: "Yale, like every other major college, is graduating scores' of bright young men ... who despise the American political and economic system."

As these "bright young men," from campuses across the country, seek opportunities to change a system which they have been taught to distrust — if not, indeed "despise" — they seek employment in the centers of the real power and influence in our country, namely: (i) with the news media, especially television; (ii) in government, as "staffers" and consultants at various levels; (iii) in elective politics; (iv) as lecturers and writers, and (v) on the faculties at various levels of education.

Many do enter the enterprise system — in business and the professions — and for the most part they quickly discover the fallacies of what they have been taught. But those who eschew the mainstream of the system often remain in key positions of influence where they mold public opinion and often shape governmental action. In many instances, these "intellectuals" end up in regulatory agencies or governmental departments with large authority over the business system they do not believe in.

If the foregoing analysis is approximately sound, a priority task of business — and organizations such as the Chamber — is to address the campus origin of this hostility. Few things are more sanctified in American life than academic freedom. It would be fatal to attack this as a principle. But if academic freedom is to retain the qualities of "openness," "fairness" and "balance" — which are essential to its intellectual significance — there is a great opportunity for constructive action. The thrust of such action must be to restore the qualities just mentioned to the academic communities.

What Can Be Done About the Campus

The ultimate responsibility for intellectual integrity on the campus must remain on the administrations and faculties of our colleges and universities. But organizations such as the Chamber can assist and activate constructive change in many ways, including the following:

Staff of Scholars

The Chamber should consider establishing a staff of highly qualified scholars in the social sciences who do believe in the system. It should include several of national reputation whose authorship would be widely respected — even when disagreed with.

Staff of Speakers

There also should be a staff of speakers of the highest competency. These might include the scholars, and certainly those who speak for the Chamber would have to articulate the product of the scholars.

Speaker's Bureau

In addition to full-time staff personnel, the Chamber should have a Speaker's Bureau which should include the ablest and most effective advocates from the top echelons of American business.

Evaluation of Textbooks

The staff of scholars (or preferably a panel of independent scholars) should evaluate social science textbooks, especially in economics, political science and sociology. This should be a continuing program.

The objective of such evaluation should be oriented toward restoring the balance essential to genuine academic freedom. This would include assurance of fair and factual treatment of our system of government and our enterprise system, its accomplishments, its basic relationship to individual rights and freedoms, and comparisons with the systems of socialism, fascism and communism. Most of the existing textbooks have some sort of comparisons, but many are superficial, biased and unfair.

We have seen the civil rights movement insist on re-writing many of the textbooks in our universities and schools. The labor unions likewise insist that textbooks be fair to the viewpoints of organized labor. Other interested citizens groups have not hesitated to review, analyze and criticize textbooks and teaching materials. In a democratic society, this can be a constructive process and should be regarded as an aid to genuine academic freedom and not as an intrusion upon it.

If the authors, publishers and users of textbooks know that they will be subjected — honestly, fairly and thoroughly — to review and critique by eminent scholars who believe in the American system, a return to a more rational balance can be expected.

Equal Time on the Campus

The Chamber should insist upon equal time on the college speaking circuit. The FBI publishes each year a list of speeches made on college campuses by avowed Communists. The number in 1970 exceeded 100. There were, of course, many hundreds of appearances by leftists and ultra liberals who urge the types of viewpoints indicated earlier in this memorandum. There was no corresponding representation of American business, or indeed by individuals or organizations who appeared in support of the American system of government and business.

Every campus has its formal and informal groups which invite speakers. Each law school does the same thing. Many universities and colleges officially sponsor lecture and speaking programs. We all know the inadequacy of the representation of business in the programs.

It will be said that few invitations would be extended to Chamber speakers. This undoubtedly would be true unless the Chamber aggressively insisted upon the right to be heard — in effect, insisted upon "equal time." University administrators and the great majority of student groups and committees would not welcome being put in the position publicly of refusing a forum to diverse views, indeed, this is the classic excuse for allowing Communists to speak.

The two essential ingredients are (i) to have attractive, articulate and well-informed speakers; and (ii) to exert whatever degree of pressure — publicly and privately — may be necessary to assure opportunities to speak. The objective always must be to inform and enlighten, and not merely to propagandize.

Balancing of Faculties

Perhaps the most fundamental problem is the imbalance of many faculties. Correcting this is indeed a long-range and difficult project. Yet, it should be undertaken as a part of an overall program. This would mean the urging of the need for faculty balance upon university administrators and boards of trustees.

The methods to be employed require careful thought, and the obvious pitfalls must be avoided. Improper pressure would be counterproductive. But the basic concepts of balance, fairness and truth are difficult to resist, if properly presented to boards of trustees, by writing and speaking, and by appeals to alumni associations and groups.

This is a long road and not one for the fainthearted. But if pursued with integrity and conviction it could lead to a strengthening of both academic freedom on the campus and of the values which have made America the most productive of all societies.

Graduate Schools of Business

The Chamber should enjoy a particular rapport with the increasingly influential graduate schools of business. Much that has been suggested above applies to such schools.

Should not the Chamber also request specific courses in such schools dealing with the entire scope of the problem addressed by this memorandum? This is now essential training for the executives of the future.

Secondary Education

While the first priority should be at the college level, the trends mentioned above are increasingly evidenced in the high schools. Action programs, tailored to the high schools and similar to those mentioned, should be considered. The implementation thereof could become a major program for local chambers of commerce, although the control and direction — especially the quality control — should be retained by the National Chamber.

What Can Be Done About the Public?

Reaching the campus and the secondary schools is vital for the long-term. Reaching the public generally may be more important for the shorter term. The first essential is to establish the staffs of eminent scholars, writers and speakers, who will do the thinking, the analysis, the writing and the speaking. It will also be essential to have staff personnel who are thoroughly familiar with the media, and how most effectively to communicate with the public. Among the more obvious means are the following:

Television

The national television networks should be monitored in the same way that textbooks should be kept under constant surveillance. This applies not merely to so-called educational programs (such as "Selling of the Pentagon"), but to the daily "news analysis" which so often includes the most insidious type of criticism of the enterprise system. Whether this criticism results from hostility or economic ignorance, the result is the gradual erosion of confidence in "business" and free enterprise.

This monitoring, to be effective, would require constant examination of the texts of adequate samples of programs. Complaints — to the media and to the Federal Communications Commission — should be made promptly and strongly when programs are unfair or inaccurate.

Equal time should be demanded when appropriate. Effort should be made to see that the forum-type programs (the Today Show, Meet the Press, etc.) afford at least as much opportunity for supporters of the American system to participate as these programs do for those who attack it.

Other Media

Radio and the press are also important, and every available means should be employed to challenge and refute unfair attacks, as well as to present the affirmative case through these media.

The Scholarly Journals

It is especially important for the Chamber's "faculty of scholars" to publish. One of the keys to the success of the liberal and leftist faculty members has been their passion for "publication" and "lecturing." A similar passion must exist among the Chamber's scholars.

Incentives might be devised to induce more "publishing" by independent scholars who do believe in the system.

There should be a fairly steady flow of scholarly articles presented to a broad spectrum of magazines and periodicals — ranging from the popular magazines (*Life, Look, Reader's Digest,* etc.) to the more intellectual ones (*Atlantic, Harper's, Saturday Review, New York,* etc.) and to the various professional journals.

Books, Paperbacks and Pamphlets

The news stands — at airports, drugstores, and elsewhere — are filled with paperbacks and pamphlets advocating everything from revolution to erotic free love. One finds almost no attractive, well-written paperbacks or pamphlets on "our side." It will be difficult to compete with an Eldridge Cleaver or even a Charles Reich for reader attention, but unless the effort is made — on a large enough scale and with appropriate imagination to assure some success — this opportunity for educating the public will be irretrievably lost.

Paid Advertisements

Business pays hundreds of millions of dollars to the media for advertisements. Most of this supports specific products; much of it supports institutional image making; and some fraction of it does support the system. But the latter has been more or less tangential, and rarely part of a sustained, major effort to inform and enlighten the American people.

If American business devoted only 10% of its total annual advertising budget to this overall purpose, it would be a statesman-like expenditure.

The Neglected Political Arena

In the final analysis, the payoff — short-of revolution — is what government does. Business has been the favorite whipping-boy of many politicians for many years. But the measure of how far this has gone is perhaps best found in the anti-business views now being expressed by several leading candidates for President of the United States.

It is still Marxist doctrine that the "capitalist" countries are controlled by big business. This doctrine, consistently a part of leftist propaganda all over the world, has a wide public following among Americans.

Yet, as every business executive knows, few elements of American society today have as little influence in government as the American businessman, the corporation, or even the millions of corporate stockholders. If one doubts this, let him undertake the role of "lobbyist" for the business point of view before Congressional committees. The same situation obtains in the legislative halls of most states and major cities. One does not exaggerate to say that, in terms of political influence with respect to the course of legislation and government action, the American business executive is truly the "forgotten man."

Current examples of the impotency of business, and of the near-contempt with which businessmen's views are held, are the stampedes by politicians to support almost any legislation related to "consumerism" or to the "environment."

Politicians reflect what they believe to be majority views of their constituents. It is thus evident that most politicians are making the judgment that the public has little sympathy for the businessman or his viewpoint.

The educational programs suggested above would be designed to enlighten public thinking — not so much about the businessman and his individual role as about the system which he administers, and which provides the goods, services and jobs on which our country depends.

But one should not postpone more direct political action, while awaiting the gradual change in public opinion to be effected through education and information. Business must learn the lesson, long ago learned by labor and other self-interest groups. This is the lesson that political power is necessary; that such power must be assidously (sic) cultivated; and that when necessary, it must be used aggressively and with determination — without embarrassment and without the reluctance which has been so characteristic of American business.

As unwelcome as it may be to the Chamber, it should consider assuming a broader and more vigorous role in the political arena.

Neglected Opportunity in the Courts

American business and the enterprise system have been affected as much by the courts as by the executive and legislative branches of government. Under our constitutional system, especially with an activist-minded Supreme Court, the judiciary may be the most important instrument for social, economic and political change.

Other organizations and groups, recognizing this, have been far more astute in exploiting judicial action than American business. Perhaps the most active exploiters of the judicial system have been groups ranging in political orientation from "liberal" to the far left.

The American Civil Liberties Union is one example. It initiates or intervenes in scores of cases each year, and it files briefs amicus curiae in the Supreme Court in a number of cases during each term of that court. Labor unions, civil rights groups and now the public interest law firms are extremely active in the judicial arena. Their success, often at business' expense, has not been inconsequential.

This is a vast area of opportunity for the Chamber, if it is willing to undertake the role of spokesman for American business and if, in turn, business is willing to provide the funds.

As with respect to scholars and speakers, the Chamber would need a highly competent staff of lawyers. In special situations it should be authorized to engage, to appear as counsel amicus in the Supreme Court, lawyers of national standing and reputation. The greatest care should be exercised in selecting the cases in which to participate, or the suits to institute. But the opportunity merits the necessary effort.

Neglected Stockholder Power

The average member of the public thinks of "business" as an impersonal corporate entity, owned by the very rich and managed by over-paid executives. There is an almost total failure to appreciate that "business" actually embraces — in one way or another — most Americans. Those for whom business provides jobs, constitute a fairly obvious class. But the 20 million stockholders — most of whom are of modest means — are the real owners, the real entrepreneurs, the real capitalists under our system. They provide the capital which fuels the economic system which has produced the highest standard of living in all history. Yet, stockholders have been as ineffectual as business executives in promoting a genuine understanding of our system or in exercising political influence.

The question which merits the most thorough examination is how can the weight and influence of stockholders — 20 million voters — be mobilized to support (i) an educational program and (ii) a political action program.

Individual corporations are now required to make numerous reports to shareholders. Many corporations also have expensive "news" magazines which go to employees and stockholders. These opportunities to communicate can be used far more effectively as educational media.

The corporation itself must exercise restraint in undertaking political action and must, of course, comply with applicable laws. But is it not feasible — through an affiliate of the Chamber or otherwise — to establish a national organization of American stockholders and give it enough muscle to be influential?

A More Aggressive Attitude

Business interests — especially big business and their national trade organizations — have tried to maintain low profiles, especially with respect to political action.

As suggested in the Wall Street Journal article, it has been fairly characteristic of the average business executive to be tolerant — at least in public — of those who attack his corporation and the system. Very few businessmen or business organizations respond in kind. There has been a disposition to appease; to regard the opposition as willing to compromise, or as likely to fade away in due time.

Business has shunted confrontation politics. Business, quite understandably, has been repelled by the multiplicity of non-negotiable "demands" made constantly by self-interest groups of all kinds.

While neither responsible business interests, nor the United States Chamber of Commerce, would engage in the irresponsible tactics of some pressure groups, it is essential that spokesmen for the enterprise system — at all levels and at every opportunity — be far more aggressive than in the past.

There should be no hesitation to attack the Naders, the Marcuses and others who openly seek destruction of the system. There should not be the slightest hesitation to press vigorously in all political arenas for support of the enterprise system. Nor should there be reluctance to penalize politically those who oppose it.

Lessons can be learned from organized labor in this respect. The head of the AFL-CIO may not appeal to businessmen as the most endearing or public-minded of citizens. Yet, over many years the heads of national labor organizations have done what they were paid to do very effectively. They may not have been beloved, but they have been respected — where it counts the most — by politicians, on the campus, and among the media.

It is time for American business — which has demonstrated the greatest capacity in all history to produce and to influence consumer decisions — to apply their great talents vigorously to the preservation of the system itself.

The Cost

The type of program described above (which includes a broadly based combination of education and political action), if undertaken long term and adequately staffed, would require far more generous financial support from

American corporations than the Chamber has ever received in the past. High level management participation in Chamber affairs also would be required.

The staff of the Chamber would have to be significantly increased, with the highest quality established and maintained. Salaries would have to be at levels fully comparable to those paid key business executives and the most prestigious faculty members. Professionals of the great skill in advertising and in working with the media, speakers, lawyers and other specialists would have to be recruited.

It is possible that the organization of the Chamber itself would benefit from restructuring. For example, as suggested by union experience, the office of President of the Chamber might well be a full-time career position. To assure maximum effectiveness and continuity, the chief executive officer of the Chamber should not be changed each year. The functions now largely performed by the President could be transferred to a Chairman of the Board, annually elected by the membership. The Board, of course, would continue to exercise policy control.

Quality Control is Essential

Essential ingredients of the entire program must be responsibility and "quality control." The publications, the articles, the speeches, the media programs, the advertising, the briefs filed in courts, and the appearances before legislative committees — all must meet the most exacting standards of accuracy and professional excellence. They must merit respect for their level of public responsibility and scholarship, whether one agrees with the viewpoints expressed or not.

Relationship to Freedom

The threat to the enterprise system is not merely a matter of economics. It also is a threat to individual freedom. It is this great truth — now so submerged by the rhetoric of the New Left and of many liberals — that must be re-affirmed if this program is to be meaningful.

There seems to be little awareness that the only alternatives to free enterprise are varying degrees of bureaucratic regulation of individual freedom — ranging from that under moderate socialism to the iron heel of the leftist or rightist dictatorship.

We in America already have moved very far indeed toward some aspects of state socialism, as the needs and complexities of a vast urban society require types of regulation and control that were quite unnecessary in earlier times. In some areas, such regulation and control already have seriously impaired the freedom of both business and labor, and indeed of the public generally. But most of the essential freedoms remain: private ownership, private profit, labor unions, collective bargaining, consumer choice, and a market economy in which competition largely determines price, quality and variety of the goods and services provided the consumer.

In addition to the ideological attack on the system itself (discussed in this memorandum), its essentials also are threatened by inequitable taxation, and — more recently — by an inflation which has seemed uncontrollable. But whatever the causes of diminishing economic freedom may be, the truth is that freedom as a concept is indivisible. As the experience of the socialist and totalitarian states demonstrates, the contraction and denial of economic freedom is followed inevitably by governmental restrictions on other cherished rights. It is this message, above all others, that must be carried home to the American people.

Conclusion

It hardly need be said that the views expressed above are tentative and suggestive. The first step should be a thorough study. But this would be an exercise in futility unless the Board of Directors of the Chamber accepts the fundamental premise of this paper, namely, that business and the enterprise system are in deep trouble, and the hour is late.

THE REAL GRAND BARGAIN COMING UNDONE
Alexander Keyssar August 19, 2011

Despite all the recent talk of "grand bargains," little attention has been paid to the unraveling of a truly grand bargain that has been at the center of public policy in the United States for more than a century.

That bargain — which emerged in stages between the 1890s and 1930s — established an institutional framework to balance the needs of the American people with the vast inequalities of wealth and power wrought by the triumph of industrial capitalism. It originated in the widespread apprehension that the rapidly growing power of robber barons, national corporations and banks (like J.P. Morgan's) was undermining fundamental American values and threatening democracy.

Such apprehensions were famously expressed in novelist Frank Norris's characterization of the nation's largest corporations — the railroads — as an "octopus" strangling farmers and small businesses. With a Christian rhetorical flourish, William Jennings Bryan denounced bankers' insistence on a deflationary gold standard as an attempt to "crucify mankind upon a cross of gold." A more programmatic, and radical, stance was taken by American Federation of Labor convention delegates who in 1894 advocated nationalizing all major industries and financial corporations. Hundreds of socialists were elected to office between 1880 and 1920.

Indeed, a century ago many, if not most, Americans were convinced that capitalism had to be replaced with some form of "cooperative commonwealth" — or that large corporate enterprises should be broken up or strictly regulated to ensure competition, limit the concentration of power and prevent private interests from overwhelming the public good. In the presidential election of 1912, 75 percent of the vote went to candidates who called themselves "progressive" or "socialist."

Such views, of course, were vehemently, sometimes violently, opposed by more conservative political forces. But the political pressure from anti-capitalists, anti-monopolists, populists, progressives, working-class activists and socialists led, over time, to a truly grand bargain.

The terms were straightforward if not systematically articulated. Capitalism would endure, as would almost all large corporations. Huge railroads, banks and other enterprises — with a few exceptions — would cease to be threatened with nationalization or breakup. Moreover, the state would service and promote private business.

In exchange, the federal government adopted a series of far-reaching reforms to shield and empower citizens, safeguarding society's democratic character. First came the regulation of business and banking to protect consumers, limit the power of individual corporations and prevent anti-competitive practices. The principle underlying measures such as the Sherman Antitrust Act (1890), the Pure Food and Drug Act (1906) and the Glass-Steagall Act (1933) — which insured bank deposits and separated investment from commercial banking — was that government was responsible for protecting society against the shortcomings of a market economy. The profit motive could not always be counted on to serve the public's welfare.

The second prong of reform was guaranteeing workers' right to form unions and engage in collective bargaining. The core premise of the 1914 Clayton Act and the National Labor Relations Act of 1935 — born of decades of experience — was that individual workers lacked the power to protect their interests when dealing with large employers. For the most poorly paid, the federal government mandated a minimum wage and maximum hours.

The third ingredient was social insurance. Unemployment insurance (1935), Social Security (1935), and, later, Medicaid and Medicare (1965) were grounded in the recognition that citizens could not always be self-sufficient and that it was the role of government to aid those unable to fend for themselves. The unemployment-insurance program left unrestrained employers' ability to lay off workers but recognized that those who were jobless through no fault of their own (a common occurrence in a market economy) ought to receive public support.

These measures shaped the contours of U.S. political and economic life between 1940 and 2000: They amounted to a social contract that, however imperfect, preserved the dynamism of capitalism while guarding citizens against the power imbalances and uncertainties that a competitive economy produces. Yet that bargain — with its vision of balance between private interests and public welfare, workers and employers, the wealthy and the poor — has been under attack by conservatives for decades. And the attacks have been escalating.

The regulation of business is decried now, as it was in 1880, as unwarranted interference in the workings of the market: Regulatory laws (including antitrust laws) are weakly enforced or vitiated through administrative rule-making; regulatory agencies are starved through budget cuts; Glass-Steagall was repealed, with consequences that are all too well known; and the financial institutions that spawned today's economic crisis — by acting in the reckless manner predicted by early-20th-century reformers — are fighting further regulation tooth and nail. Private-sector employers' fierce attacks on unions since the 1970s contributed significantly to the sharp decline in the number of unionized workers, and many state governments are seeking to delegitimize and weaken public-sector unions. Meanwhile, the social safety net has frayed: Unemployment benefits are meager in many states and are not being extended to match the length of the downturn; Republicans are taking aim at Medicaid, Medicare, Social Security and Obamacare. The real value of the minimum wage is lower than it was in the 1970s.

These changes have happened piecemeal. But viewed collectively, it's difficult not to see a determined campaign to dismantle a broad societal bargain that served much of the nation well for decades. To a historian, the agenda of today's conservatives looks like a bizarre effort to return to the Gilded Age, an era with little regulation of business, no social insurance and no legal protections for workers. This agenda, moreover, calls for the destruction or weakening of institutions without acknowledging (or perhaps understanding) why they came into being.

In a democracy, of course, the ultimate check on such campaigns is the electoral system. Titans of industry may wield far more power in the economic arena than average citizens, but if all votes count equally, the citizenry can protect its core interests — and policies — through the political arena. This makes all the more worrisome recent conservative efforts to alter electoral practices and institutions. Republicans across the nation have sponsored ID requirements for voting that are far more likely to disenfranchise legitimate (and relatively unprivileged) voters than they are to prevent fraud. Last year, the Supreme Court, reversing a century of precedent, ruled that corporate funds can be used in support of political campaigns. Some Tea Partyers even want to do away with the direct election of senators, adopted in 1913. These proposals, too, seem to have roots in the Gilded Age — a period when many of the nation's more prosperous citizens publicly proclaimed their loss of faith in universal suffrage and democracy.

Alexander Keyssar is the Stirling professor of history and social policy at Harvard's Kennedy School and the author of "The Right to Vote: the Contested History of Democracy in the United States."

DR. JAMES R. LEUTZE

Under the dynamic leadership of Dr. James R. Leutze, the University of North Carolina at Wilmington strengthened its undergraduate teaching and overall academic excellence to become one of the top 10 public regional undergraduate universities in the South. It became recognized nationally for its marine biology program and internationally for its technological initiatives in global learning.

During Dr. Leutze's tenure, enrollment rose from nearly 7,000 students to approximately 10,600. Even as UNCW's admission standards rose, the number of freshmen admitted continued to grow.

Under his leadership, the university successfully completed its first capital campaign in 1998, raising $25 million for scholarships, professorships and programs supporting UNCW's educational and service missions. The university's endowment grew from $4.8 million to nearly $21 million, and the operating budget increased from $58.8 million to more than $134 million.

Likewise, the campus itself grew during Dr. Leutze's tenure to include more than 90 classroom, residential, administrative and support buildings. It continued to grow over the next several years as UNCW undertook its largest construction effort ever using the $108 million higher education facilities bonds approved by voters in 2000.

A native of Charleston, S.C., Dr. Leutze holds a bachelor's degree from the University of Maryland, a master's degree from the University of Miami and a doctoral degree from Duke University. He served in the U.S. Air Force, rising to the rank of captain, and worked as a legislative assistant for Sen. Hubert Humphrey.

As a professor of history at the University of North Carolina at Chapel Hill, Dr. Leutze was recognized for his excellence in undergraduate teaching. He was named chair of the Curriculum for Peace, War and Defense and, in recognition of his teaching and research, was appointed the first Dowd Professor of War and Peace. Prior to coming to UNCW in 1990, Dr. Leutze was president of Hampden-Sydney College.

Dr. Leutze created the international affairs program, Globe Watch, which aired for 15 years on public television networks nationally and internationally. Four public television documentaries were produced by the university as a result of his deep interest in addressing environmental issues and their global implications for economics and society: River Run: Down the Cape Fear to the Sea, Treasure Coast: The Natural Heritage of the North Carolina Shore, Currents of Hope: Reclaiming the Neuse River and Paving the American Dream: Southern Cities, Shores and Sprawl.

Dr. Leutze was a prolific researcher and writer. He has published numerous books and articles on international affairs and national security, including Bargaining for Supremacy: Anglo-American Naval Collaboration 1937-41 and A Different Kind of Victory: The Biography of Admiral Thomas C. Hart.

Under Dr. Leutze's leadership, UNCW initiated several technological advancements to take a leadership role in the global learning society of the 21st century. These initiatives and the university's emphasis on regional and global outreach and the development of partnerships provided the basis for UNCW's involvement in a virtual university pilot project with Japan and other countries. He was appointed by former Gov. Jim Hunt to lead the Digital Communities Project that was spearheaded by the Japanese Industry Development Association, several university presidents and governors of prefectures in Japan.

The governor also appointed Dr. Leutze to chair the N.C. Rural Internet Access Commission, a 21-member group that makes recommendations regarding efforts to provide economically depressed areas with high-speed Internet access. Dr. Leutze was a member of the North Carolina Progress Board and served on the board of directors of the Kenan Institute-Asia, the Daniel D. & Elizabeth H. Cameron Foundation and the Donald R. Watson Foundation. He was a trustee of the George Marshall Foundation.

As chancellor, Dr, Leutze built a firm foundation for the university to grow and excel as it met the challenges of the 21st century and the increasing demand for quality higher education.

Made in the USA
Lexington, KY
17 December 2014